I0461579

It Was Her

A Memoir

HARPER A. BAILEY

Copyright © 2025 by Harper A. Bailey Published in the
United States by: DreamHer Inc.

All rights reserved. No part of this book may be repro-
duced by any mechanical, photographic, or electronical
process, or in the form of a phonographic recording;
nor may it be stored in a retrieval system, transmitted,
or otherwise be copied for public or private use—other
than for "fair use" as brief quotations embodied in
articles and reviews—without prior written permission
of the publisher.

Disclaimer: This book is a memoir. It reflects the
author's present recollections of experiences over time.
Some events have been compressed and some dialogue
has been recreated. Some names and characteristics
have been changed.

Book Cover by Taylored Design Group

ISBN: 978-8-9998966-5-0
1st Edition
Printed in The United States of America

Mom, you are the reason.
JD, thank you for saving my life and reconnecting
me to my purpose.

Cinco, you will always be the best part of the
sandwich.

For Emory, the little girl in me deeply admires
and sees you as a superhero.

To my life partner, Cliff, thank you for embracing my
capacity before completely falling in love with my
potential, which has enabled me to soar higher than I
could've done alone.

"Life can only be understood backwards; but it must be lived forward."

—Soren Kierkegaard

Contents

Part 1 — Running

Part 2 — Falling

Contents

Foreword

For nearly thirty years, I have stood in front of millions of people all over the world and helped them realize that they, too, have the power to transform their lives.

It's been a humbling and inspiring thing to witness. In room after room, conversation after conversation, I've seen people connect with the hope that they had previously filed away. I've watched them walk away taller and stronger, choosing the conviction of their truth over the convenience of their pain. And all of this through simply sharing my story.

Stories are powerful. When we mine the moments in our lives, we discover a treasure chest of opportunities to turn our mess into our message. We uncover our strength, our adaptability, our determination. We come to know our resilience, and we see evidence of triumph after triumph.

It's why I was drawn to Harper's book and why I wanted to write this foreword. Like you, she has a Unique Soul Message that she weaves together through memorable, potent moments of her life. And just so we're clear—life gave her plenty of content, plenty of opportunity to be a victim instead of a victor. And yet, she chose healing over comfort. Harper's story speaks to the power of not giving up, of being willing to push for more. I saw myself in these pages; I was taken back to my own defining moments. Her struggles were a portal to my own strength, and they will be for you as well.

When you read this book, I encourage you to remember your own power to choose. At any given moment, we all have the choice to fall backward or push forward. We may not always know how we're going to take the next step, but we can decide that we're going to find a way to take it.

I didn't know how I was going to buy diapers for my son Jelani all those decades ago standing in front of that ATM with only eleven dollars and forty-two cents to my name. All I knew was that I would create a better future, no matter what it took. That one moment, that one story, has spring-boarded me into a life and a career beyond my wildest dreams.

Now, I have the privilege of speaking to people all over the world. And I've seen time and again what it looks like when a message really gets through. I can see that exact moment when the logic combines with the emotion, and the magic happens in someone's mind. You see, people will respect you if you take them to their head, but they'll remember you if you take them to their heart.

Harper has written a book that you will both respect and remember.

She has woven together a tapestry of moments from her life that will stay with you long after you close these pages, long after you've forgotten the exact details or the specific date. You'll remember how you felt when you read them. You'll remember her breakthroughs, her power. And because of that, you'll believe it's possible for you too.

You get to design your destiny. You get to choose the life you lead.

May *It Was Her* remind you that it was always you.
You were always the answer you were seeking.

Lisa Nichols
Founder and CEO, Motivating the Masses
New York Times Bestselling Author of *No Matter What*

All A Dream

Her presence hung in the room even after I awoke.

A tad tipsy, I forced my brain to make sense of the nightmare that had jolted me from sleep. I rubbed my thumbs across each palm, certain the rope burns would be etched in my skin. My lungs felt heavy and worked over.

I walked my mind back through each image.

The dream had begun like any other. I could see my adult self working hard, meeting deadlines, my eyes set on the next big thing that caught my attention.

In my grasp, a frayed rope strained between my hands. It was worn and splintered—one end tethered to a shiny horizon while the other threatened to slip through my fingers. It felt heavy in my palms, a reminder of the unyielding expectations that plagued me.

With the rope taut and my hands trembling, I sprinted forward, heart pounding like a drum, my breath coming in quick bursts, an echo of willpower that felt almost reckless. I quickly understood that this wasn't an ordinary race; it was a marathon. The track was my life, and the challenge increased with each mile achieved.

But as I ran, I realized I wasn't an adult anymore.

I had morphed into a version of my younger self, and I was desperately fleeing from something that was chasing me—something that I couldn't quite make out. As its menacing presence stalked me, I gasped for air, exhausted from building as much distance as I could between my assailant and me.

When I looked over my shoulder to glance at how far I'd come, I caught a glimpse of the blur behind me as it sharpened into a haunting figure.

It was me. I was chasing myself.

Her eyes were wide with despair, a silent plea across her tear-streaked face. There she stood—a ghost of my past—her shoulders trembling, hollow breaths attempting to push out a scream, desperation transmitting from her body. Worn down by all she'd experienced, this girl was trying to catch up to me.

PART 1:

Running

CHAPTER 1:

The Beginning of the End, Again

"Your mother has something to tell you," my aunt said urgently.

It was June 2013, and I had been busy at work in my office when my aunt's call came through.

"Here, tell her!" she ordered as she passed the phone to my mom.

My mom's tearful voice struggled through the line. "Hey, Ma, what's going on?" I asked.

"Tell her," my aunt insisted in the background. There was a long pause.

"They say I have cancer."

My breath caught in my chest, and I placed a hand on the desk to steady myself.

Mom had been struggling with health issues for a while now—namely breathing troubles, lack of appetite, and coughing spells. Her primary care doctor had assured us that, since she was a nonsmoker, she was only experiencing side effects of sarcoidosis, a condition that hadn't caused her problems in over ten years.

She had been reluctant to seek further answers, but after much pleading and several emergency room visits, she had agreed to a lung biopsy. We knew cancer was a possibility, but I don't think any of us were expecting this.

"I'm on my way." I hung up the phone abruptly, my heart racing.

My hands shook as I gathered my things, silently left my office, and sought a moment of refuge with a colleague. I collapsed into her arms, sobbing as I shared the news, and she held me tightly. After what felt like hours, I composed myself and headed out for the forty-minute drive to the hospital.

It was stage four lung cancer. Mom began treatment immediately, and I did my best to carry on and push the worst-case scenarios from my mind.

Four months into her care, I was celebrating a friend's birthday when I received another call from my aunt. "Your mom is having trouble breathing. I've turned up her oxygen, but it's not working. She's still uncomfortable," she reported. I wrapped up dinner and headed to my mom's house. When I arrived, she was asleep and reluctant to go to the hospital. She had endured countless emergency room visits, CT scans, MRIs, and chemotherapy sessions over the past few months. She was exhausted—tired of it all. We agreed to wait, and I drove her to the ER the next morning.

The admitting doctor was blunt. "Ms. Goss, there's nothing more we can do for you," he said. "We are moving you into hospice care." He explained the next steps casually, saying someone would come to have her sign some papers, and then she would be moved to another building. "I'm sorry," he added before leaving.

Distraught, I followed him out. I needed more

information. It was time to ask the questions my heart had not been ready to face since Mom's diagnosis.

"Doc, can I have a moment with you?" I asked. He turned to me, my anxiety swelling. "How much time do I have left with my mother?"

He paused, "Do you want the truth?" I nodded.

"If I were in your shoes, I would want the doctor to be honest with me too," he continued. "Your mother is very sick. Her heart rate is extremely high. She has a few days at best. Her body can't sustain much longer. Go back in there, and make memories. The hospice facility will make her comfortable until she transitions."

I thanked him and hugged him tightly before he left.

I turned back to my mother's room and watched through the window in the door as she opened the "Whopper with all the toppings" she had requested. Her appetite had been almost nonexistent recently, but she had decided to indulge.

I went back into the room and watched her eat, trying to memorize her features, hoping this painful memory might bring comfort in the future.

As the doctor mentioned, a nurse came in with stacks of papers for us to sign. "Now, what about resuscitation, Ms. Goss? Would you like to be resuscitated in the event that you become unconscious while in our care?"

"No," she said resolutely. "Mom? Really?" I was shocked.

Her voice softened, "I'll let them bring me back if that's what you want."

I saw the sadness in her eyes, and my heart sank. I grabbed her hand and said, "Mom, you don't have to do that. It's okay to go."

It happened in an instant. Just like that. Before I fully grasped the weight of my words, I had let her go.

She looked at me, "I'm just sorry that I won't be here to experience all the good things coming to you all." She squeezed my hand and then turned back to the nurse, "Please keep my answer as no."

My uncle fell to his knees, overwhelmed by the situation. My mom, firm in her decision, told him, "Get up, God's will be done. Stop that crying. Enough now!"

My uncle continued to sob softly while the rest of us remained silent. My mind raced.

How had she made her decision so quickly? Was she ready to die? We had never discussed this before; how did she know, but I didn't?

That first night of hospice stay was surreal. The room's decor featured various shades of green. The pale tile floor, once shiny, was now dull. The air smelled stale, reminiscent of mothballs. It was both clean and musty.

After Mom's diagnosis, she had been very private, only sharing her illness with those she chose. My dad was not among them. She mentioned wanting him and others to remember her when she was her vibrant self. My parents hadn't been together for nearly twenty years, but they still held something special for one another in their hearts.

That night I made dozens of phone calls to inform family and friends about her hospice admission, including my dad.

"Punkin, why didn't you tell me?" he asked, puzzled by the news.

"Dad, I respected her wishes and kept her illness private," I responded firmly.

I could hear the pain in his voice, and for a brief

moment, I felt for him. I had created a lot of space between my heart and my dad. In fact, I had been angry with him for a while. And still, I recognized the importance of including him.

For several hours, my dad, family, and friends poured through the doors, one after another. There were lots of tears and hugs. When my youngest son, Cinco, came running into the room with his boisterous energy, my mother screamed with joy. In my heart, I knew that while she didn't want him to see her in the hospital, she wanted to experience the joy his presence would inevitably bring.

It was like a scene out of a movie when Cliff's parents brought him into the room. He let go of his grandmother's hand and yelled, "Nanny!" In response, she shrieked loudly. They exchanged a long embrace. He had come into this world with a bang two years prior and brought with him the spirit of a giant.

Cinco, unaware of the occasion, sat on the bed with my mom while memories of the good times were shared. At times the room would fall into silence, only to be interrupted by laughter. I witnessed my mom looking around the room. She seemed relieved. I can't explain it, but it seems like she had accepted that her time had come, and she was ready.

It was me. I wasn't ready. I was afraid of death.

As a kid, I had been dragged to funerals where people were jumping inside of the casket and screaming with excruciating pain. I would sit there confused and scared. There was so much that I didn't understand. *What happens when someone dies? Will I die too? How can I live forever?*

My mom would always, unprompted, talk to me about her wishes for cremation and not to waste too much money celebrating her life. She was passionate about living a life full of quality and never got hung up on the quantity of years she had on this Earth. She would say, "Cremation is best for me; I will never look this beautiful dead." I would shush her, shutting those thoughts out of my mind. My mom had to live forever. Even as a kid, I knew my life would never be the same if she died.

In the months leading up to my mom's hospice stay, she had started shrinking into a shell of her extroverted self. Her smiles came only so often. Anyone who has witnessed what cancer can do to a loved one knows the helplessness that comes over you. For many nights, she cried and prayed, asking God to take the pain away. I, too, would join in on the prayer, asking God to save her.

The body that had given us and her so much joy was self-destructing. She was adamant about who prayed over her and protective of who occupied space with her. So, when I picked up the phone to call my dad that night in hospice, without informing my mom, it was a big deal. While they had spoken over the phone a handful of times that year, my mom had never shared her condition with him. I could always tell when she was talking to him because of the deep belly laughter that erupted and shook the room. He was able to give her some levity, even if he didn't know what she was going through.

She would also take calls from her siblings and close friends. One friend, Diane, would have my mom listening intently for hours at a time without barely saying a word. It would be years before I would understand how important those calls were.

People flowed in and out of Mom's hospice room

that night. It was close to midnight before it was just my uncle, my eldest son JD, my partner Cliff, and me in the room with my mom. We had decided to take the first night, making the couch, floor, and recliner work amongst the four of us.

By this time, my mom had started to fall into a deep sleep, and her breathing appeared labored. She was still working pretty hard to move air. I chose the recliner nearest her bed so that I could hold her hand. Every few minutes, I called her name to see if she was still with me, with us.

"Mom?" I'd whisper. "Yeah," she'd reply.

Each time, tears flowed from my eyes. At one point, I could no longer stop crying, and I fell onto my mom's bed. Jill, the hospice nurse working the night shift, walked in and started gently rubbing my back. Her touch felt comforting.

"Your mother has lived a great life; I can tell," she said. "She's had guests coming to see her all night, and you all are spending the night with her.

"I've been here for many years, and I've seen patients with zero guests, dying with no one by their side but me," she continued. "I've been trying to leave hospice for the last two years but can't seem to land a new role; I guess it's my ministry. It's important work, but also very hard work. I can see when someone has lived a full life with love, like your mother.

"Cry. Let the tears fall. They will fall. Cry because you will miss her, but don't cry because of regrets because you have none."

The tears that had stopped to take in Jill's message began falling again. Her words touched my heart and seemed guided by a higher power.

I was intrigued and taken by her wisdom and calm.

Struck by this being our first encounter, I was in awe of how she was able to capture and understand what I was going through. It was as though God had sent an angel to console me.

Jill stopped speaking and shifted focus to my mom. "Her breathing is getting worse. Let's see what we can do to make her more comfortable," she said.

I nodded as she left the room to find the doctor. Returning after a few minutes, she shared that the medications would be changed and assured us that she would keep working to ensure that my mom achieved comfort.

The next thing I remember, I woke up on the couch and found a handwritten note from Jill.

Thank you for being patient with us last night as we worked to make your mom comfortable. This is a bit of an art for us sometimes. Remember, no regrets because you have none.

—Jill

I looked over to my mom and saw her resting peacefully. In my heart, I knew she was making her transition to the other side. My mom never opened her eyes nor spoke again after that night.

Later that morning, a new hospice nurse visited the room, "It's almost time," she reported gently.

She suggested that we decide the order in which we would say our goodbyes. As my mother's only child, my family looked to me to go first. My partner, Cliff, had just left to be with his family at a nearby hospital, as they, too, were saying goodbye to a dear cousin on life support.

I entered and looked at my mother's still form. The

room was dim despite the morning light. Two large windows with mint-colored drapes were pushed aside, letting in a little of the sun's soft glow.

I gazed at my mother's face, once full of life. Her high cheekbones and fair skin had given way to a very narrow face. Her nose was perfectly centered between her dark brown eyes, now small slits. Her eyes used to sparkle when they caught the light.

My mother had a way of illuminating a room with her beauty, confidence, and vibrant energy. She commanded attention, and everyone knew it. Her personality was both fierce and tender, and her infectious gap-toothed laugh always made the room feel lighter.

Now, this lively woman, my hero, lay on her deathbed. Her life was slipping away with each labored breath. Each short inhale was followed by a longer, more difficult exhale, reminiscent of the pauses between ocean waves heard at night. Time seemed to crawl, and I wished desperately to rewind it. Instead, I stood over my mother as she transitioned into the afterlife.

The nurse had told us that hearing would be the last sense to go, so I held her hand and leaned in to speak into her ear. Tears streamed from my heart to my mouth, and my mind raced for the right words. This was the last time I could speak to her, wasn't it? I needed to tell her she was loved.

"Mom, I miss you already, and still, it's okay to leave.

You've given me everything I need to move on in this life. I don't know how just yet, but I will learn to live without you by my side. Your grandsons will be well taken care of and will never forget who you are and what you meant to us all. I love you, I love you, I love you."

It's incredible how we can find strength in the face of the unimaginable.

I walked out of my mom's room after saying goodbye. She was still breathing. JD and a cousin were the last ones to go in. After a few short minutes, my son came running out of the room yelling, "She's gone! She just took her last breath!"

Dashing toward the room, I stopped in my tracks when my eyes caught the sight of her body. I could see from there that life had slipped away from her face.

Steady streams of tears flowed down my cheeks as JD recounted his experience—how he had told my mom how much he loved her and that she was free to leave.

"I kissed her on the forehead, and she took her last breath. It was like she waited for me," he said.

I hugged him tightly, and we cried together.

Afterwards, I grabbed my phone and typed the message to family and friends that I never wanted to send:

The moment you know your life is about to change and there's nothing you can do about it. She's gone.

My mom was fifty-nine years old when she died. On October 6, 2013, at 10:25 a.m., she breathed her last breath. I was only thirty-three years old, and in that moment, I felt the weight of irreversible change enveloping my life.

CHAPTER 2:

Before There Was Me, There Was Her

Five years had passed. My mother had left me to navigate this world without her, and I had no say in the matter. I had done my best to suppress grief and adapt to my new reality.

During these five years, avoiding my problems had become a default mode, much like a computer operating system running in the background without notice or mention. I had a partner I loved, healthy children, a great home, and a solid job. I was even pursuing another degree. But I was running on fumes, and I couldn't comprehend why life had suddenly become increasingly challenging to manage.

Why wasn't I happy yet? I had ticked off all the boxes that society said I should, constantly moving on to the next achievement while waiting for happiness to join the party. I struggled to sustain moments of joy.

This internal conflict spurred my decision to try something new. With a face adorned in makeup and a body clothed in a new outfit in the midst of a busy workday, I sat down on the couch opposite another Black woman.

As she returned from closing the door, she met my gaze and asked, "So, tell me why you are here."

My spirit plummeted. Damn. There was nowhere to run.

Her name was Lucia—a sharpshooter with a voice filled with both kindness and intrigue. I'd often schedule therapy sessions in the middle of my workday, come in with a full face of makeup, and leave looking like a distressed, female version of the Joker.

Our early sessions started with questions about my mom, who she was to me and what I thought was driving my sadness. I later learned that Lucia diagnosed me with anxiety and adjustment disorder after our very first session, but I wasn't ready to face that yet.

"Before there was me, there was her," I began.

My mom was one half of a fraternal twin duo, born on March 23, 1954, in Detroit, Michigan. Her twin, who would become affectionately known as Auntie, was born twelve minutes earlier, making my mom the third child of the bunch. I don't recall my mom ever sharing much about their time in Detroit.

She was six years old when my maternal great-grandmother stepped in and moved the family to Ashtabula, Ohio, a small town about 50 miles outside of Cleveland. She had grown weary of hearing details about the arguments and physical abuse between my grandparents and had decided to take action.

In 1960, the population of Ashtabula was about 26,000, with only 9 percent of its residents being Black. My mom often talked about being the only Black kid in her class, where the teachers made sure that she and my aunt were never in the same classroom, despite the number of times they changed schools. According to the last count, my mom went to five elementary schools from kindergarten through eighth grade and graduated from Ashtabula High School in 1972. In her early twenties, she'd leave this small town for city lights and adventure in Chicago.

Ashtabula's small size was one of the things that made it great and also one of those "knowing each other's business" kind of towns. Getting in trouble in the neighborhood also meant getting in more trouble when you got home because Ms. Whatshername had already called your mom—not only to tell what you did but also how she whooped your behind.

To my mom, this small town felt like a warm hug on a sunny day when playing blocks away from your home. It was here where she went to church with her grandmother every Sunday and stayed until what felt like Monday.

Attending church until the age of seventeen was a mandate enacted upon my mom and her siblings and enforced by my great-grandmother.

She spoke fondly of her childhood and the place that eventually became home to seven children—six girls and one boy. My grandmother's stern ways kept the household in order. Everyone had a role, and there were clear-cut rules to be followed. Failure to follow the rules would almost certainly result in some sort of punishment.

My mom talked to me about the teachings of God that engulfed her childhood and later sent her running away from church in early adulthood. She found her way back to the house of the Lord in her mid-forties and became adamant about me seeking God on my own terms.

She'd say, "Salvation is for the one seeking it." Her beliefs have been influential behind why I've never been baptized and why I visit churches of various religions, but never sealed the deal with becoming a member.

My mom rarely talked about her dad, except when asked. He never joined or visited the family in Ashtabula. To her, my grandfather was both loving to the children and abusive to my grandmother. There were several incidents when he would come home from work intoxicated and ready to fight. Sometimes my grandmother didn't feel up to the challenge to fight back. However, there were times when that wasn't the case.

There's a story of my grandfather coming home one day and my grandmother expecting him to be angry. So she locked the doors and turned on the stove to boil water from the kitchen sink. Some short time later, she could hear him yelling outside. She ushered the kids into the basement and told them to wait there.

My grandfather broke the front door window, and as the story goes, just as he was able to open the door, my grandmother was there with the pot in her hand. She managed to pour the scalding hot water all over him, sending him screaming and retching with pain. His siblings would later say that my grandfather had received third-degree burns over two-thirds of his body.

By the time I was old enough to inquire about who and where he was, it had been nearly three decades since the last time my mom had seen him. She recalled him showing up at the school playground where she was playing with a couple of her siblings, which was a common occurrence. He'd pop up and ask the kids to go with him, even while he was still living with them. My mom's innate connection to her dad cradled her decisions to go with him most times, while her other siblings would often choose to stay behind.

Their last interaction was different. My grandfather showed up with his usual request for her to go with him. But something was off. My mom shared how, even at the age of five, she sensed the suspicion in his voice and decided not to go.

Sometime in the nineties, Auntie got curious and wanted to learn about what happened to my grandfather after the family left Detroit. His siblings filled in some details about the various states where extended family resided. They said that perhaps looking into those places might provide some intel about his whereabouts. They maintained that he had ceased communication with them too.

Social security records later revealed that payments had stopped, which most likely meant that he was deceased. His last known address was somewhere in the state of California. Weary of the pursuit, Auntie ended her investigation efforts.

Reflecting on my mom's childhood journey, I wonder how much her dad's absence impacted her. I think about how it shaped her relationships with men, and how maybe his presence, even more than his absence, influenced her protective nature over loved ones.

She was the protector. My mom was the person that her siblings would run to whenever there was trouble at school or in the neighborhood. She would be called upon to settle the score, and through her actions, it was evident that she cared deeply about family and took her sister responsibilities quite seriously. My mom would always say, "I don't start trouble, but I don't have a problem with finishing it."

She had a way of making everyone around her feel safe in the event that something would jump off. By most people's standards, my mom was a small woman—standing 5'2" and weighing 110 pounds. However, her small stature was never a limiting factor in her capabilities to defend herself and others.

As a small child, I was keenly aware of her protective nature. Thinking back, she said things that still ring in my ear to this day like, "If you are ever in danger of being kidnapped, don't go to the second location because I may not be able to find you."

And, "If anyone messes with you and says they will hurt you if you tell me, tell me anyway, and I will kill them."

I legit believed her.

I still chuckle when I think back to my ten-year-old self in the fourth grade. Compared to my mom's guts, I had none. I was seriously scared of my shadow. There was a girl named Latisha Winter, who was the same age as me on paper but resembled a seventh grader that bloomed early. She had hips, sizable boobs, and bullying tendencies.

My bestie Kia and I got in her crosshairs and became her verbal punching bag, to the point where threats were fired almost daily. Shit, I was scared.

Kia lived across the street from me. She was small in stature like me with caramel complexion and doughy, dark brown eyes complemented by perfectly shaped eyebrows. Her childlike innocence came to life with her high-pitched voice and contagious laugh. Her short, black hair was wavy and quenched with Care Free Curl activator. I was obsessed with getting a Jheri curl and begged incessantly without success. My mom was convinced that this hairstyle was only for adults.

My friend and I met in third grade, both the only children in our families. We held similar interests, like playing video games, crushing on boys, and spending copious amounts of time with each other.

Walking home from school one day, we decided that enough was enough and that we were going to jump Latisha. Fuck it. We even managed to rope in an innocent bystander, a mutual friend, into the plan.

"If she messes with us tomorrow, we'll let her know that it's on after school," I said.

My bestie was going to confront her first, and then I would join in. Our other friend was designated as backup in case things got out of control.

Fast forward to the next day. The fight lords were thirsty for some action because Latisha started calling names as we stood in the morning line waiting to go inside the school.

"I can't stand your scary ass," she said with a nasty glare. Instead of ignoring her, I stuck with the plan. "We are fighting after school today," I said before a lump formed in my throat.

Her fiery eyes lit up—it was showtime.

All I had to do was tell my girls that the alarm had been sounded and remind them of the plan to meet on the blacktop behind the school building after the bell rang. There, we'd gather the crowd and find a spot a few blocks away from school to avoid getting caught. Why not follow the typical elementary school fight protocol laid out by others?

Plan aside, my stomach churned with anxiety for

the rest of the day. What if we lost? What if she hurt me?

My thoughts raced, but outwardly, I hyped up my friends about the upcoming fight. "I can't wait to beat her ass and get this over with."

When the school bell rang, I grabbed my backpack and headed to the schoolyard, preparing for my first fight. The crowd quickly gathered—kids always loved watching a fight.

As we walked to the designated spot, we exchanged heated words. "I'm sick of you. I'm going to beat you up today," I said, surprising myself with my newfound courage.

The circle of spectators closed in on us as the tension grew. Kia confronted Latisha, getting in her face. It was our mutual friend that stepped into the circle and delivered the first punch.

Frozen in place and unable to move, I became a mere spectator. I watched as the girls exchanged blows, with no clear winner emerging, until a teacher's voice pierced through the chaos, yelling, "Cut that out!" We all scattered.

Breathing a sigh of relief, I realized I'd narrowly escaped a dangerous situation. Now, all I had to do was make it home. I needed to run. As I sprinted away, the noise of the crowd grew closer. When I glanced back, I saw Latisha charging towards me like a bull, her eyes locked on her target.

Like a deer in headlights, my body stiffened and my mind blanked before I noticed that I had been saved once again when Kia stepped in between us. Latisha struck Kia in the chest and grabbed her by the shirt collar, swinging her around in a circle.

Suddenly, there was a loud noise as Latisha

slammed Kia's head into a pole. The sound of her face smacking metal jolted me into a full-on sprint until I reached the fence surrounding my back porch. Eyes locked downward, I skipped steps as I bolted up the three flights. With shaky hands, I unlocked the door and threw myself inside to safety.

Thank god Mom is at work, I thought. My mind raced, trying to find the right sequence of words that would convince her to switch my school in the morning. There was no way I could face anyone at that school again.

My breathing quieted just enough to hear an unexpected noise coming from inside the apartment. My ears pricked up as my stomach dropped. I knew that sound. My mother emerged from her bedroom before she came into view.

Why was she here? And why was she wearing a robe?

No words were spoken as she scanned my body and sensed the fear that I was desperately trying to mask. This wasn't her first time dealing with such situations, having faced similar challenges with her own siblings.

"What's wrong?" she asked sharply.

I hesitated, unable to confess that I had run home from a fight. My mother always encouraged me to stand up for myself and never let bullies win.

"The best way to deal with a bully is to stand your ground," she often said.

"You never bring a fight home; it's not safe. Don't provoke conflicts, but if they arise, finish them. Bullies need to know they can't mess with you. They may not stop bullying altogether, but they will leave you alone. Don't make me come up to that school," she'd warn.

As I rose to my feet, I could hear chatter from outside growing louder. The crowd had followed me home. My heart sank, weighed down with panic.

A perceptive smirk formed on my mom's face. She ordered me to move from the door and then flung it open. She stepped outside and surveyed the crowd below the porch before calling out, "Who's here to witness a fight?"

I nearly collapsed on the kitchen floor. The crowd roared with excitement. Then my mom said, "Who wants to fight my baby?" There was a brief pause before she yelled, "She will be right down."

My eyes widened in disbelief. *Had I heard her correctly?* There was no way I was going back down into the lion's den. My mom ordered me to change my shoes and take off my gold hoop earrings.

I began pleading with her, "Aren't you supposed to call the principal? Shouldn't you call her mother?"

Blatantly ignoring my pleas, she disappeared as she walked back to her bedroom.

"Pull your hair back," she said after returning fully dressed. Following her instructions, I prepared to face the impossible. With my shoes tied tightly, I stood up and walked to the door with my mom holding my shoulders. I descended the stairs, my mom behind me. Before reaching the pavement, she said, "Don't worry, I won't let anything happen to you. Do you trust me? If you keep running, they will keep chasing you. It's time to confront the problem."

Outside of the wire fence, Latisha's piercing stare penetrated my soul. I got the feeling that the long wait fed her anger and intensified her intention to kick my behind. My mom stepped into the middle of the crowd with me close behind her and declared, "This will be a one-on-one fight. No one else can jump in, and when I say it's over, it's over."

She stepped aside, and before I knew it, my fists

were clenched tightly by my face as I moved towards Latisha. I swung my arms as fast as I could. I felt some punches land on my body but kept swinging with my eyes tightly squinted.

After seeing enough bloodshed, my mom yelled, "That's enough! Now everyone go home now. And don't ever come back here for a fight because next time I won't be as nice." She abruptly turned and followed me back up the stairs.

My heart was pounding so loudly that I could both feel and hear it. I just had my first fight. I didn't win but was proud that I threw some punches.

My mom's reassuring words lifted my spirits even more. "See, I told you everything would work out. Now, remember never to chase anyone home for a fight, and no more running."

The next day, I went to school with my head held a bit higher than the previous one. As weeks passed, Latisha and I slowly became acquaintances. We even played Double Dutch together after school sometimes.

This was one of the many times my mom came to my aid, teaching me how to stand up for myself. She had been my vigilant protector for thirty-three short years, and after her death I was left to face life alone.

The shock of her passing bled right into the surreal task of planning her memorial service. I wasn't ready to say goodbye in the presence of others; I wanted to be alone. Being around others made her death feel too real. There was no denying the finality of it all that I felt in my heart.

She was no longer here to protect me, uplift me, laugh with me, or walk beside me through life's challenges. This was the end, and everyone knew it. I was alone.

The shift in how I experienced life after her passing hit me suddenly and intensely. Even in a room full of people talking, I found myself only catching bits and pieces of the conversation. I was easily distracted by any and everything that appeared to be more interesting. The struggle to stay engaged was real. My now-dulled senses made close sounds seem distant and vibrant colors muted. I felt like a mere shell of the person I used to be, yet I was tasked with finding a way to move forward in life.

Even today, I find it incomprehensible how society keeps moving forward when someone dies. Depending on your employer, the amount of time off you receive is tied to a societal-driven, terribly flawed system that ranks your relationship with the deceased. There is little room for personal grieving once the services are over. After the calls and visits cease, you are expected to pull yourself together and carry on with your life.

In keeping up with the norms placed before me, I fuddled through memorial service planning with a scattered brain leading the way. There was so much to do, and I was determined to hold the service within a week. This sense of urgency guided my actions. I was at the funeral home the next morning after my mom's passing, followed by a visit to church to work on the service details. Announcements to family and friends went out by end of day.

The planner in me kicked into high gear and provided enough distraction to avoid facing the reality of my mom's death. The endless list of tasks to complete helped to conceal the sharp pain I felt when walking into my mom's bedroom with her no longer lying there. I kept myself busy throughout the week, adding more tasks as each day passed.

I had to write the obituary, get it printed, figure out what to wear, and decide how the church would be decorated. Everything had to be perfect. This is what she would have wanted.

Cliff and I barely talked about anything else other than the service during this time. He did his best to hold me whenever I sat still enough and let the emotions hit me. And in return, I made sure that these uneasy moments were fleeting. I hated how the feelings of hopelessness and uncertainty made me feel empty.

So I kept moving past them and finding something tangible to focus my energy on. Something else that I could control, like the repast menu. My mom liked sweets, so I needed to make sure that there were several options to choose from.

Interestingly enough, outside of being clear about wanting to be cremated, my mom hadn't provided any specifics on how she wanted to be honored. So I went with what I thought I knew—a celebration held and experienced by loved ones at her church home, stellar gospel singing, and kind words spoken from the pastor and attendees.

And lots of hugs.

My mom loved hugs and gave them away freely, where the embraces mirrored her mood. The warmest hugs included both arms, involved your hearts touching, and lasted long enough to seize the moment.

The night leading up to the service was a long one as I placed my deep purple dress on the hanger. After Cliff and the boys went to sleep, the silence was deafening. I wondered about my ability to get dressed and walk out the door in the morning. Would I even be able to do it?

I tossed and turned through the three hours

of sleep that I managed to get. Rolling out of bed, I mustered enough energy to combat the hesitation and fog weighing me down. It took me at least two hours to get dressed and neatly apply my makeup.

Looking at myself in the mirror, I started an inner dialogue trying to prepare how I would look, feel, and act that day. My plan was to just hold it together. I felt some comfort knowing that my mother had been cremated and there would be no body to face lying in the casket. No caked-up makeup to cover the scars, no wig on her head to conceal the hair loss. There would only be twelve-by-eighteen-inch pictures of her on display in the church hallway and sanctuary. A picture slideshow would be playing on the large-screen TV over the pulpit, so I could see my mother laughing and living life on her terms.

My mother's memorial service was held on Friday, October 11 at her church home—five days after her passing and two days after her cremation. At least a hundred or more friends, family, coworkers, and loved ones came to celebrate the life of Jeannette Goss.

Climbing the church steps after exiting the family limo is a memory that will remain intact in my brain forever. It was my turn to be a part of the immediate family procession.

I distinctly remember walking down the church aisle and seeing the blurred sea of sad faces staring at me and mouthing their condolences. The hugs were plentiful and heartfelt as I made my way down the mile to the front pew. My legs never felt securely under me; it was as if my knees had given out. Cliff held me up and kept encouraging me to put one foot in front of the other.

My dad successfully closed out the tribute by

sharing how he met my mom on her way to work. "I saw this fine, bowlegged woman walking down the street. I had to pull over. You know, and one thing led to another, and you see my beautiful daughter sitting right there," he said while pointing to me.

His hands clutched on either side of the podium. He paused to take a breath that eased his shoulders a bit. "I'm going to miss her. If I had to give her a score, it would be a nine point five out of ten." The crowd exploded with laughter, and a smile crossed my face that helped to remind me of the love that my parents had for each other.

Grateful to have survived the service, I was stopped on the way to the repast being held in the basement. It was Mom's friend Diane, her face draped with sorrow. I was anticipating her presence but hadn't seen her until now. I turned to receive another warm hug. Through tears, she expressed her condolences and how much she was going to miss her friend.

"That was my girl. Boy, we had some times together. I wanted to catch you and tell you to please give me a call when you are ready to talk. I want to share some details from the many conversations I had with your mom before she passed away. There are things that I believe you would want to know," she said.

Other attendees began to join us at the top of the stairs, waiting to go down. I nodded in acknowledgment of her request. I felt no curiosity stirring within me and figured that I would reach out to her one day.

Little did I realize, it would take nine whole years.

CHAPTER 3:

It's Complicated

"Please stop hitting her!" I screamed as loud as my four-year-old lungs could muster.

I scanned the park looking for help.

"Somebody, please help us!" Hot tears streamed down my face as panic set in, and I realized that no one was coming to our rescue.

"Help!"

Punch after punch, the angry man pummeled the lady who had kindly taken me and his two daughters to the park to play that summer afternoon. Cars rolled by with nosy adults peering through their windows at the violence taking place, but no one stopped to help.

It was the first time I remember witnessing a man physically harm a woman.

The woman was well-known in the neighborhood as someone without kids of her own but who was great at caring for them. She had come to our house earlier that day to ask my mom if she could take me and a couple neighbor girls to the nearby park. My mom had happily agreed and requested that I be brought home before it got dark outside. The lady took my hand, and we proceeded to walk a few doors down to see if two sisters who were close to my age could join us.

The girls were outside as we walked up to their house. "We are heading to the park, do you all want to come?"

she called out.

The girls jumped with excitement. "You have to ask our dad first," they instructed.

We all walked through the gangway–the pavement that sits between two buildings–leading to the back of the house and the alley where their dad was working on a car. He was so preoccupied with fixing the car that it took a moment before he realized we were there.

"We are heading to the park. Can your daughters go too?" the lady asked.

The man craned his head out from underneath the car hood. "Make sure you have them back before dark," he barked. Before we could turn to head toward the park, he had buried his head back under the hood.

We skipped and laughed the entire way. This park visit was glorious—we flew down the slide, soared on the swings (my favorite thing to do), and chased each other around until we got tired. As dusk began to rear its ugly face, the lady gathered us to leave. We all held hands on the short walk back home.

As we were nearing the next block, a menacing figure stalked towards us. It took a moment for it to move close enough for my little eyes to recognize that it was the girls' dad.

His fists were balled up, and he was yelling unintelligible words our way. His strides were long and steady as the distance between us got shorter and shorter.

The girls and I stopped in our tracks as the lady kept walking toward him. His finger was pointing at her as the screaming continued. His anger had distorted his image; he no longer resembled the dad we had left earlier. Rage had swallowed him whole.

"You took my kids! You stole them!" His fists were getting tighter, and the muscles in his neck started to swell.

"But we came...to ask you..."

Before the lady could finish, he hit her in the face. She flew backwards, coming completely out of her sandals as she grabbed her face in shock.

He charged at her again and continued to throw punch after punch. At some point, he backed off. She rolled around on the ground holding her sides. Skin scraped by the pavement, she bled onto the sidewalk.

I stood frozen, unable to take my eyes off the lady.

Terrified tears streamed down my face. The girls' screams finally snapped me back into reality. We shouted for help and tried to wave down cars. No one came.

"That's all I remember," I said, reopening my eyes after replaying the memory during a session with Lucia.

She looked at me with curiosity in her eyes, "And what happened next?"

I shrugged my shoulders trying to bring my body back into the room, returning back to the present. It was as though I had been teleported back in time to relive this awful memory.

This would happen often in our sessions. We would be talking about when I first experienced a particular feeling or thought. And after some scrolling through my mental rolodex, I'd close my eyes and share whatever came through first. This particular memory had bubbled up after Lucia had asked me to think back to when I initially realized that I was scared of men.

The way she phrased her request had stunned me. Up until that time, I had not explicitly told her that I was scared of men, only that I hated them. Bringing fear into the chat unlocked a new door to explore in my mind and memories.

Lucia was no stranger to my many issues with men. We had spent much time in our sessions talking about my strained relationship with my father, in particular.

My dad was born in June of 1952, in Donaldson Point, Roseland—a small town in the Mississippi Delta. He had been named after the famous boxer, Joe Louis, and smiled when people made the connection.

He was number six in the lineup of eight children—four boys and four girls. I only know a handful of details about my dad's childhood days.

He completed school through the eighth grade and, up until that time, worked early mornings on the farm before the school bell rang. As a kid, he'd often tell me about how he would get up as early as four a.m. to handle tasks given to him by his dad—my grandfather— who tragically died in a head-on collision when my dad was only eighteen.

The impact of losing his dad (or anything about his dad, really) was never something we talked about. I had only learned about the car accident while overhearing a family member bring it up in my presence as a young teen. By my dad's account, his childhood years were hard on him, and he felt as though he was the black sheep of the family and mostly misunderstood by others.

In spite of the challenges experienced as a child and through adolescence, my dad was a popular cat that had a way with words, a nice smile, and a charming effect on the ladies. When he wasn't fixing whatever he could get his hands on, he could be found capturing the attention of others and tilting the room with laughter with his witty jokes. The ladies loved Joe and chased him down for as long as he could remember.

Smiling while talking, he'd say, "I can't explain it; they just loved me, Punkin. I couldn't keep them off me. I don't know what it is." Punkin was the nickname my dad gave me and was later adopted by his side of the family.

Maybe it was his short, stocky build, evenly dark chocolate skin tone, and bowlegged walk that made the ladies want to get to know him. Or maybe it was his almost-shoulder-length Jheri curl hairstyle and country boy accent in a happening city like Chicago in the early seventies that brought all the girls to my dad's yard. Like my mom, he relocated to Chicago in his early twenties.

My parents met in 1978 at a popular shopping store that would be the equivalent to Target today. She was walking the aisles looking for something, unaware of my dad watching her from afar. To this day, my dad still beams when he tells the story.

"Your mama was fine, baby. I had to ask for her number. I needed to know who she was. So, I shot my shot. She was blushing when I approached and asked for her name. She glanced down at the frisbee in my hand and asked who it was for. I told her that I was buying it to play with my kids. Her eyes lit up, and she told me that she admires a man that spends time with his kids. Asking for her number came next, and the rest is history."

Sometime shortly after meeting, my dad shared

that he had two children. My mom would later learn that the real number of children he had fathered at that time was indeed six, with several of them residing less than twenty miles from the place they would eventually share together. The brood eventually grew to nine, including me, although I was the only child he shared with my mom.

The early years of their relationship were filled with laughter and fun. My mom talked about how my dad courted her and made sure she felt cared for. They went on dates, hung out at parties with family and friends, and wore matching leather outfits.

My dad was a motorcycle enthusiast and longtime member of a local club with several chapters across the states. My parents experienced the winds smacking their helmets as they cruised down long stretches of highway headed to places near and far, like Atlanta and Myrtle Beach.

"The road trips were always so fun. There would be hundreds of bikers riding in formation," my mom would tell me many years later with a blissful grin on her face as she reminisced about the early days.

She enjoyed riding on the back of my dad's motorcycle so much that she put a brand new seventy-eight Kawasaki on layaway so that he could teach her how to ride. The riding lessons eventually paid off because my mom not only embraced her new skill set, but became an avid rider in the process.

The freedom she experienced in her twenties preoccupied her interests and squashed her dreams of being a mom. For her, there was too much appeal in being able to go where you wanted when you wanted and spend your money on whatever piqued your interests.

Her mind changed abruptly after learning that she

was pregnant. This knowledge brought along with it giddy visions for her future that included having a boy and naming him Kunta Kinte just like the actor from her favorite show, *Roots*. She'd joke about calling him Kunta for short just to get a reaction from others.

I still cringe at the thought of that being my name if I had been a boy. The name-calling would have been nonstop. Family members still laugh to this day about the many conversations that were had to sway her. If it had not been for me being a girl and no viable girl names at the ready, I don't think that my mom would have ever relinquished her rights to my godmother, who named me.

By the time I arrived in 1980, my parents were on rocky terms. I am told that my father didn't attend the birth but came to visit sometime later.

I never got the chance to ask my mom about what transpired in their relationship. However, I do know that my parents loved each other deeply and lacked the knowledge to work through challenges that came their way. Their relationship underwent cycles of being on and off for decades, until my mom decided to be done when I was sixteen years old—the same year my dad would tell me a secret that would rock my entire world.

CHAPTER 4:

Ground Zero

I was born via C-section at a community hospital on the west side of Chicago, about five minutes from where Auntie and my mom shared an apartment. My mom liked to remind me how I was almost two weeks past my due date and had forced her tiny frame to gain almost fifty pounds. Pregnancy had pushed her to her limits so much that she never wanted to experience it again.

Childhood pictures reveal the adoration in my mom's eyes when looking at me. These pictures serve as firm reminders of the pride that my mom had in knowing that I was hers to care for.

Even though she originally had her heart set on a son, she leaned into being a 'girl mom' and dressed me up like a baby doll well into my formative years. Everything had to coordinate from my head to my toes. If the dress was pink, the socks and shoes were required to be white. I'd even have matching beads and hair ties to complete the look.

We left the city for a bordering suburb, Oak Park, a tree-lined community with more diversity, a mix of apartment buildings, and homes with character. Here,

I could attend better schools and have the continuity that my mom longed for as a child. Ultimately, I'd live on the same street for two decades. We did move once, but it was only to the building next door.

I became a latchkey kid by the second grade. My mom worked long days far from our home, which made it nearly impossible for her to take me to school or pick me up.

Interestingly enough, I don't have any pictures of my dad and me before the age of ten. He was around, spending nights with my mom and me at the apartment, but he also had his own home separate from us. Sometimes we'd pack our bags to stay the night at his house. His place felt cold and unwelcoming to me. I spent most of my time alone in the spare bedroom trying to rock myself to sleep, praying for the morning to come so I could go home.

His disinterest in being my dad was obvious. There were no questions asked about my favorite color or the types of things that I liked to do. Instead, we connected through his interests.

My dad was really good with his hands. He was a self-taught carpenter that could fix anything. I watched him work on cars, motorcycles, and toilets. I've even seen my dad knock down a wall and build it back up.

He owned a door-hanging business in the early nineties, and I'd go on jobs with him during the summer. We rode together in his non-air-conditioned, two-door truck to hang a door or do some other odd job. My role was to observe, pass tools, and ask tons of questions.

"Dad, why did you screw that thing in there like that? I would not have done that," I would warn.

"Punkin, see this is how you do this and this," he'd explain.

He exhibited more patience and attention towards me when we were alone. When my mom was within earshot, he would go out of his way to be critical of my behavior and command that I do more. My grades were never good enough, my room was never clean enough—it was always something. Because of this, I nicknamed him Mr. Perfect.

To Mr. Perfect's disliking, I hated elementary school.

The teachers were boring and mean. I enjoyed making new friends and liked the idea of learning, but social studies, math, and English could go jump in a lake. I only wanted to learn about things that interested me, like art and reading. I would talk and distract other students when the boredom set in (which happened on most days), which inevitably landed me in trouble with my teachers.

Despite the stories that I told myself about how well I did in school, my grades and the teacher's comments on my report cards reflected my behaviors quite accurately. *Good student overall. She has more potential and talks too much,* they would write over and over again.

The scoldings weren't enough to sway me to do the right thing for longer than two days. I would tell myself how much I wanted to do better and felt like I could, but school just wasn't for me.

Being a fourth grader was a complete nightmare. The class was tasked with learning the names of the United States presidents from someone who clearly had never been young before—the infamous Ms. Shar. She was an older woman and reminded me of a witch. She had all the classic features—old, scraggly gray strands hanging from her head, black clothes, and long, pointy fingers. In my dreams, she tortured her students and made them study with dark, fiery rings surrounding them. I was convinced that she had it out for me.

Boy, was I right.

I nearly failed that year because of her and Super Mario Brothers. I received a Nintendo for Christmas and fell into a gaming coma. I played in the dark under the covers after my mom went to bed and every day as soon as I got home from school. Homework became an afterthought, as did studying.

"Have you finished your homework?" my mom would ask.

"Yup, all done," I would yell back with my eyes fixated on the screen. "Just one more level," I would whisper to myself.

By the time the third quarter rolled around, I felt a knot in my stomach during the parent-teacher conference. Ms. Shar's words hit me like a slap. "If she doesn't improve these grades, she's going to need to repeat the grade. There's still time."

My mouth fell to the floor as anger moved through me, mixed with a hint of betrayal. Why hadn't she warned me? I glanced at my mom, her body tense, radiating with disappointment. The air in the room felt charged and heavy with unspoken fears.

That night, I faced the consequences of my mom's wrath as her frustration boiled over and she yanked the plug from my beloved Nintendo, nearly breaking it. The console laid abandoned on the floor, a silent testament to my failure.

Luckily, my academic performance wasn't all there

was to tell about who I was. From an early age, music was my refuge, where I could lose myself in the powerful lyrics and melodic tones of my favorite artists. Michael and Janet Jackson rocked my world nonstop. Their *Bad* and R*hythm Nation* albums became the soundtracks to my life. I'd beg my parents for money to buy not only their albums, but also magazines like *Right On* and *Teen Beat*. My bedroom walls transformed into a shrine of posters, each one a look inside of a world that I longed to escape to.

Lying in my bed, I spent time staring at their images, imagining their perfect lives filled with fashion, fame, and glamor, whispering to myself, "One day, I'll be rich too." All I needed to do was grow up and get out of this house.

I held simple beliefs that were foundationally based on young-person logic. I wholeheartedly believed that only bad things happen to bad people and that only good things were for good people. So, living as an adult like the rich and famous made sense to me.

In my eyes, everything had to be fair. If something wasn't fair, I would become easily frustrated and ready to make my case to make it just. All occurrences had to make sense to me in order for them to be accepted, and I could move forward.

Injustice smacked me squarely in the face at the age of eleven when my dad moved in with my mom and me. It was a huge deal. Before, when he would come stay with us, I could look forward to him leaving for his house and me having a place of refuge away from him. Now, I would have to contend with him every day.

Even though I moved out of my mom's room and into one of my own, our small apartment got even smaller when he arrived with his things. My dad must have sensed my dismay because he came in guns blazing with new rules, "Your room needs to be cleaned every day. There will be no dishes in the sink at night. You will knock when coming to our room."

I was astonished by my mom's restraint in allowing him to take control. This place had been hers to rule until Napoleon arrived and marked his newfound territory with hot skunk piss.

The limited privacy I had before his arrival vanished before my eyes. I felt like a prisoner who hadn't committed any crimes but was forced to pay the price. My bedroom door couldn't be closed without permission but could be opened at any time without advance notice. Furthermore, my quarters were subject to a strip search without a warrant.

My dad went to extreme lengths to assert his dominance. The punishments became more frequent, lengthier, and came with awful terms. Oftentimes, my phone privileges would be revoked. Being on the phone with friends was a favorite pastime, and taking it away was the equivalent to having nothing. They could've taken everything out of my room and left the phone. I would've gladly slept on the floor without a blanket, if it meant that I could still talk on the phone for hours.

This addiction was my Achilles heel, as I was sure that I would die if I couldn't be on the phone. I snuck to make calls whenever my parents left the house. There was no way that I would miss out on the gossip taking place after school.

My dad, convinced that it would only be a matter of time before I broke the punishment rules, placed a tape recorder under my bed and overheard my conversations.

This act not only extended my punishment but also angered my mom when she heard the derogatory names I used while venting to a friend on the phone. Ironically, it was my dad that saved me from that beating.

Another punishment for bad behavior in school landed me in my parents' prison for an entire summer, during which I managed to read all the books in the *Sweet Valley High* series. This unfortunate occurrence, however, helped to ignite my thirst for reading. Hours slipped away as I got lost in books and my strong imagination teleported me to different places or periods in time. Closing my eyes helped to clearly see the setting and dip inside a character's adventure or despair.

Auntie gifted me my first diary after seeing how my zest for reading gave way to a new passion–writing. Equipped with a gold-plated lock and key, I vowed to write daily, divulge all my secrets, and keep it forever.

Over the years, it became a trusted advisor of sorts and my way to process what was happening in my life. I'd chronicle about how my dad's stay slowly ate away at the space between him and my mom, space they desperately needed to cool off in between arguments. The frequency of their arguments increased and created a growing tension that lingered in the air like smoke. The source of their challenges initially didn't interest me, but I couldn't bypass the shifts in my mom's demeanor.

Her frustration was sticky like mud and felt unavoidable. She became more irritable and complained about things that wouldn't normally upset her, like the long commute to work in the morning or a cup being left in the sink overnight. Over time, I watched my mom shrink and become a quieter version of her boisterous self.

This shift helped to feed the resentment that was already building up inside me. I became an angry child who harbored resentment towards my dad for his lack of interest in me. I found him to be mean and narrow-minded, often belittling me with comments like, "Kids should stay in their place," and "You're just a kid; what do you know?"

What I truly wanted was a father who would listen, support my interests and dreams, and show love unconditionally. I wanted a father who wouldn't verbally or physically punish me for mistakes or for not meeting his expectations.

I longed for a father who would embrace my quirks, offer hugs, and routinely express his love. I wanted him to protect me like my mom did and prioritize my wellbeing. The little girl in me wished for the shelter that only a father's love could provide.

As time passed, I became disappointed in my mom for allowing him to control our lives at my expense. The limited time I did get alone with her was enjoyable; the space felt safer and more predictable. She was livelier and more open to hearing my thoughts when it was just us, even asking, "Can I have a penny for your thoughts?" Each time she asked, I felt a sense of importance, knowing that she cared enough to listen to me.

Being an only child was the best of both worlds. I sometimes relished the solitude, and other times, I was bored to death of my own existence. I often begged for friends to visit, only to treat them poorly with my possessiveness over my toys. Most playdates ended in arguments, with my friends leaving disappointed.

The cycle of solitude, play, and itch for companionship continued into my teenage years.

Like many other only children that I knew, I had all the cool toys, and lots of them. You name it—Barbies, Cabbage Patch dolls, Sega, Nintendo. The list goes on.

I spent the months leading up to Christmas watching all the toy commercials and thumbing through both the Sears and Spiegel catalogs. A lengthy list would be crafted, and on Christmas, Santa and Mom would deliver the goods. I had no understanding of the lengths that my mom would go to make it all happen. Like clockwork, magic struck every Christmas, birthday, and several days in between.

All of this felt normal to me and created an attachment to material things early on. In my mind, when the friends left, I still had my things. There were times when these things filled me, and times when they didn't, especially when chaos in my home was in peak season.

I can see now all the ways that I found to cope with the parts of life that I didn't understand and how those small adaptations in childhood grew to gaping holes in adulthood. They created their own minefield, but instead of tiptoeing around bombs, I was carefully dodging all the uncomfortable truths I had pushed away. And with one wrong step, I'd go tumbling into darkness.

CHAPTER 5:

Fathering Secrets

I was either twelve or thirteen when I stumbled from the bathroom to the kitchen in the middle of the night to grab a glass of milk. I had been asleep and woke up thirsty.

I was comfortable moving about the house in the dark and could navigate with my eyes closed. I grabbed a glass from the top cabinet with my right hand while opening the fridge door with the other. Holding the glass with both hands, I gulped down the milk until the silence was broken.

"Punkin, you see this?"

Startled by my dad's voice coming from the dark side of the kitchen, I dropped the glass. The room stood still for a moment as I spun around to see my dad sitting at the kitchen table just five feet away from me, holding a flashlight. On the table were emptied containers of spices from the kitchen cabinet, arranged in tiny sand-like piles. He had dumped the spices and was examining them for something.

For months leading up to this moment, my dad had been working overtime to tell anyone who would listen that my mom was trying to poison him. He was clear in his assertion.

"She's not trying to kill *you*; she's trying to kill *me*," he would say while pointing at his chest.

These claims had come headfirst into our lives without warning or cause, and with their arrival came a turn for the worse in my family dynamic. I had started to grow weary of my dad's hurtful assertions and became increasingly uninterested in being alone with him. And yet, here we were in a dark kitchen, me half-asleep and half-naked in my T-shirt and panties.

Hearing the glass shatter on the floor snapped me back into the moment. I needed to respond but wasn't sure what I could say that would hurry this interaction and make it any less uncomfortable.

I took a deep breath as I closed the refrigerator door, the flashlight now the only light interrupting the darkness. Pretending to be interested, I walked over to the table to glance at what he was trying to show me. Maybe there would be something this time. Perhaps I would finally see what he had been so desperately trying to warn me and so many others about.

Several of my aunts and my grandmother had been brought into this imaginary bubble where my dad held all the answers. I was saddened that he was still searching for the smoking gun to prove his point, and I silently prayed that he would just stop—stop blaming my mother for any wrongdoing (because she didn't have the capacity to kill him) and stop involving me. I wanted out.

All I could see under his flashlight were small mounds of grains neatly placed on the table. Nothing suspicious caught my eye. Trying to maintain my composure and give him a chance to explain himself, I asked, "Dad, what do you want me to see?"

My dad lifted his gaze from the table and looked me in the eyes. His enlarged pupils held a soft sadness, prompting me to examine the rest of his face. There were beads of sweat forming around his graying hairline. His dark skin looked worn and glossy. Even though I was looking at the physical man that was my dad, he wasn't truly there.

The softness in his eyes turned into panic. "You don't see this?" he yelled, using the flashlight to point at the table.

"Dad, I'm sorry; I don't see what you are trying to show me. I'm really trying."

His tense shoulders slumped downward, defeat settling over him.

It was time for me to get out of that kitchen. If history were to repeat itself, I would either be met with anger or pleas for help. I was never able to handle either reaction or come out unscathed. *If I could only make it back to my room and close the door, this would all be over*, I thought to myself. So, I said the one thing that I knew would blow this whole thing up.

"Mom isn't trying to kill you!" There, I'd said it.

He looked back up from the table at me again, this time with tears in his eyes. Until then, I don't recall ever seeing my dad cry.

I felt nothing.

I turned my back and left the kitchen. For me, this situation was over. I didn't want to be involved. I knew I just needed to keep my distance from him and not engage.

The silence followed me into bed, where I laid in disbelief, heart pounding outside of my chest. The man sitting in that kitchen was not my dad. He was not the dad that I both hated and loved. Nor the dad who showed me how to fix things and how to drill screws into wood. The kitchen guy, with sweat dripping down from his temples, was someone else entirely.

How could this be? What happened to the guy I knew?

My anxiety-warped thoughts were sprinting at the speed of light, unable to make sense of what was happening.

My dad could never give a logical reason why my mom might be trying to kill him. My mother vehemently denied all of my dad's accusations. She'd tell me, my dad, family, and friends how deeply she loved him and how she would never harm him.

I believed her. Both my heart and my mom needed me to. Looking back at all that she had done for me, I had to be an ally. It only made sense. And I had to believe that despite my dad's delusions, he was choosing to stay because he also deeply loved my mom.

His stance defied all logic for me and evaporated what little trust I had in him. The distance between us grew at an exponential rate in the days following that night.

Until he was ready to be honest about whatever was happening, I was resolved to create more distance. This subtle estrangement traveled into my thirties, where I could easily let several months go by without calling. I made it a point not to answer his calls and to ignore the many messages sent to me through my mom, urging me to contact him. The story I told myself was that this was my only option and that he was responsible for what happened to us.

I spent much of my early teen years trying to find my people at school and listening to my parents scream and argue each night about the woes of their relationship. The walls between our bedrooms were too thin.

When my mother wasn't blaming my dad for not contributing his share of the bills, she was yelling at him about marriage. "Why won't you marry me? Don't you want to be with me forever? I am the only sister in my family who hasn't been married yet. What are you waiting for?" she would ask with desperation in her tone.

My father often responded dismissively, which only made my mom angrier. "I don't want to get married now. I don't care what your sisters are doing. Good for them."

My mother wasn't the only one not fitting in with the "in crowd." I was a late bloomer compared to my friends—being the last to get my period and develop enough boobs to meet the threshold for my mother to buy a training bra.

"Not yet, babe," my mom would say as she peeked under my shirt.

Did God forget about me? When would I grow up and become a woman? I needed this childhood stage to hurry up. I desperately needed a body to attract the fellas— only the girls that possessed them kept their attention.

I was boy crazy! Everything about them was intriguing—from how they smelled to how they walked. I liked fresh haircuts and clean sneakers. Dreaming about having sex preoccupied my thoughts, especially when I was supposed to be paying attention to the teacher.

My mind was filled with images of what "it" would be like, what they would do, and how I would react. In my head, sex was a magical experience that would take me to another world of ecstasy, where my body would feel things I had never experienced before. A diary entry at thirteen years old read:

My sex life is nonexistent. I'm just at that peak where I think about having sex at the perfect moment with that special someone. It all seems like a fantasy.

My obsession with sex and boys was definitely connected to the music and television I was consuming. I can still sing the lyrics to "Stay" by Jodeci from front to back. I was enamored with songs about love—everything from the courting period to breakups and even make-ups. It was as if sex came with a money-back guarantee, and I wanted in, pun intended.

Soap operas in the nineties were also a big deal.

Watching them with my mom and grandma gave me an idea of what love would be like—a lot of drama, money, and lovemaking. I had also managed to get my hands on some porn at a friend's house, and those actors made sex seem like a funky time.

Sadly, the boys had little to no interest in me, making middle school both boring and overall uneventful. All my relationships were short, lasting a couple of days to a few weeks at best. The arguments were plentiful, no matter the duration. I was always nagging them about something.

"Why didn't you sit next to me at lunch? Do you like her more than me? Hey, you didn't call me back like you said you would."

It felt like I was always being let down, and the boys had an agenda to get in my pants. And to my own surprise, I was more interested in being a voyeur and singing about sex than actually doing it. The fear of moving beyond French kissing scared me, even when the opportunity to advance to third base presented itself. I became like a cat, always landing on my feet with some excuse to get me out of the hot seat.

Somehow, turning sixteen and finding myself unexpectedly single (again) caused an interpersonal shift in me. Ego and apathy had stepped onto the dance floor, and anger had become the DJ. I went from trying to figure out why people were betraying me to centering my desires.

I was fed up with trying so hard to fit in at school, making friends, and losing them over arguments about who was the "most right."

The time had come to live on my terms. I had grown tired of the moving targets and people-pleasing. Those situations left me teary eyed and with another scar across my heart. Something had to give.

My new frame of mind was to have a "fuck-it" attitude. I began to notice how much more I liked myself than I did before, which then made me more inclined to keep moving in this direction. I prioritized my wishes, like wanting more than just a relationship, but a situation that provided some security with someone who cared about my interests too. And if they couldn't do that, then I would move on.

I was on a mission to get what I thought I needed to feel whole because I'd come to realize that something was incomplete within me. Something that I couldn't put words to.

Unfortunately, my home life had not improved one bit either. My parents eventually got engaged, but the happiness never settled in for either of them. After years of begging to be married, my mom's engagement to my dad lasted only six months before she told him to leave. She threw in the towel on a relationship that had taken up close to eighteen years of her life. Maybe she realized that they could never reach the mountaintop that she had dreamed about for so long.

My dad's erratic behavior never ceased, and he became a radically different person in the five years we lived together. After he was gone, my mom was stern in her instructions to not answer the door for him if he came by. It was no longer safe to have him in the house, and she wasn't sure what measures she would need to take to protect us if push ever came to shove.

One night when I was sixteen years old, my mom was away from home working the third shift, and there was a knock at the back door. It was around eight o'clock, and I was with a friend playing kitchen beautician. She was applying thin layers of oil to my scalp and hairline perimeter to protect it from the burn that'd follow after the perm cream set in.

There shouldn't have been any unexpected visitors. Our apartment complex was surrounded by a ten-foot locked gate. You had to have a key or follow someone else in if you wanted to access the property.

I paused for a moment to see if the knock would return before making the decision to answer. The banging returned, this time with a few more thumps than the first.

"Who is it?" I yelled through the door.

"It's me, Punkin. Open the door. I need to talk to you." I hadn't seen or heard from my dad since his forced departure months prior. Panic crept up my body; I had a decision to make. I could disobey my mom by opening the door and hearing him out or tell him no and walk away.

He, of all people, was keenly aware of my mom's

wishes for him not to come back here. Why would he put me in this position? I knew how betrayed my mom would feel if I opened that door.

"Punkin, I really need to see you," he insisted.

I couldn't leave him out there. I opened the door, intently surveying him as he walked into the kitchen. He was wearing a dingy army fatigue jacket and jeans. His hair was out of place, strands going in every direction but downward. His hands were shaking, and the urgency on his face saddened me. Something was wrong.

I sat back down to continue with my hair appointment but kept my eyes on his small frame standing in front of me.

"Punkin, I miss you. I need to tell you some things. I need you to hear it from me. Some things have happened. I'm so sad. I miss you. I miss your mom."

His voice was shaking as he continued, "I've been really down—like really down. I felt like I was running out of options, so I tried some things that I've never done before."

The pauses in between his words prompted me to ask, "Dad, what did you do? Tell me, please." We only had a handful of minutes before I would be telling him to leave.

"I tried crack, babe. I tried it and didn't like it. I felt like I had no other choice."

Shock ran through my body, and thoughts started taking over, making it hard to hear what else he had to say.

"So, you tried it? Are you still trying it?"

"Yes, Punkin. I am so low. I told you. I don't know what else to do. What else can I do?" He was crying now, pleading for me to respond.

My thoughts swirled. *My dad is doing drugs, and he wants me to know. Why does he want me to know? What can I do?*

"Punkin, I am hurting so bad. I wish I could die right now. I wish I could eat that perm and just die."

My friend chuckled in the background. She had been quiet the whole time—other than reminding us that he couldn't stay long—and her reaction hurt. Nothing about this was funny.

Sadness consumed me. In a million years I never could have imagined this was the important message my dad had to share with me. I felt like I was drifting out of my body, my mind shuffling through all the many moments when my dad's behavior had changed from the man I knew.

My friend nudged me, snapping me back to reality. "Dad, you have to leave."

I had heard enough. This was more trouble than I could bear. He wasn't supposed to be here.

"Dad, you have to leave. I won't tell Mom; I promise." His pleading intensified. "Punkin, I'm hungry and cold.

I don't have anyone. Can you help me?"

He started fidgeting with both hands in his pockets and pulled out a pack of raw hot dogs. In an instant, one disappeared into his mouth.

I couldn't believe what I was witnessing. *How had my dad gotten himself into this situation? How had we all gotten here?* There was no time to sort this all out; he had to leave now.

I leaned in for a hug. It was all that I could give. His body felt foreign and smaller than I remembered. We held each other for a brief moment. I could tell that he didn't want to release his embrace, but the time had come for him to go.

Neither of us could ever speak of this visit again. I was worried about how my mom would respond to me disobeying her orders. And I knew I wouldn't be able to find the words to repeat what he told me anyways. The gravity of his admission was heavy like cement blocks, so I decided to bury it—to make it go away to the place where I kept the other secrets.

"Dad, I'll call you," I lied as I closed the door behind him.

I wouldn't call him until a year later. But not because I wanted to help him. This time I was the one with a secret to share.

PART 2:

Falling

CHAPTER 6:

She's Gotta Baby

Most mornings, I woke up and headed straight into the bathroom to strip naked and examine my changing body in the mirror. It was the spring of 1998. I was eighteen years old, and my distended belly was now accompanied by swollen ankles and white pimples of varying sizes dotted all over my face. My once-tiny, uncurved body had ballooned as it carried a baby boy right before my eyes.

My thirty-nine-week and four-day pregnancy had flown by for me—likely because I did everything I could to pretend that I wasn't a pregnant teenager. I went out as much as possible, trying my best to avoid my mom's objections. "You need to sit your behind down," she'd say. "Nothing better happen to my grandbaby. You hear me?"

I can see now how much denial I was in. I tried to move forward like life could stay the same. I found a new boyfriend, and we successfully dated for about four months before he learned about my situation. The layers of lies to keep my secret were numerous and sometimes downright lazy. I was always on my period, wearing baggy clothes, and directing where and how his hands could touch my body. The disappointment on his face when he found out still stings. I didn't feel for him one bit back then, but now I can admit to how deceitful I had been.

I met my baby daddy, Kiren, the previous summer before senior year outside Kids Foot Locker as I waited for a friend to finish her shift. I had taken a train and bus to the mall to buy some shoes using her discount and was promised another bonus—a ride home from her mom. "Girl, hurry up," I pleaded through the caged gate as she placed shoes back on the shelves and vacuumed the burgundy carpet.

My head swiveled when Kiren and his friend entered the main hall and started walking toward me. His golden skin and matching-toned jewelry immediately caught my attention. He wore large cubic zirconia studs in both ears, pinky rings on both hands, and a gaudy watch on his left wrist.

They walked right past my overzealous stares.

My homegirl dropped the vacuum mid-stroke and ran over, yelling, but trying to be discreet, "Girl! He's cute!" Hearing her outburst, Kiren turned back around and locked eyes with mine. I was smitten.

It wasn't until they walked back my way a few minutes later that I noticed his perfect black curls, fresh lining, and hazel eyes. My friend was right; this boy was cute! He had a swagger that was unfamiliar to me, and he was smooth and deliberate with his words. He asked for my name and number and then walked away saying, "I'll give you a call."

I tapped my hip to make sure my beeper was still in place. I waited impatiently for the page that came three days later.

Our first interaction outside of the mall was chaotic.

He picked me up with another friend in the car, and I realized quickly this wasn't a real date. We rode around the west side, smoking weed-filled blunts and rapping to the new Twista album, *Adrenaline Rush.*

It turned out that we'd never be alone unless we were having sex. There were no deep kisses or bodies moving in sync like they did in the movies. I had been sexual with two other guys before our situation, and with them it felt like I'd imagined. There was passion. They'd ask what I liked, and I'd bring my lips to their ears and whisper, "Kiss and rub my neck." Not with Kiren.

His disinterest in getting to know me didn't bother me at first. I didn't care that my attraction to him didn't translate into mind-blowing sex. I just wanted to be around him.

There were times when he'd open up and share light details about himself.

"I have a sister and some brothers; my parents are married and have a house."

He had what I assumed was his own car. He had graduated from high school in 1997 and said he maybe wanted to go to college one day.

The girls really liked him too. His pager sounded off all the time, and he'd disappear to make a call, often coming back distracted and ready to rid himself of me.

We carried on seeing and sleeping with one another for the next two months before I realized that I had the same number of tampons in my backpack as I did after my period ended in July.

It was mid-September.

My brain did somersaults. There was no way I could be pregnant. Had I really messed up this soon? My sex life had just launched. I was only seventeen.

This doesn't happen to girls who had been told by their mothers not to have sex. There was no way I could be pregnant; I mean, I'd only had unprotected sex about ten and a half times.

"It's positive," said the woman at the Catholic-funded pregnancy testing clinic three blocks away from my high school. The shock that ran through my bones made my hands sweat.

"Can I take another test? Maybe that was wrong."

She sat down next to me on the faded floral loveseat and put her right arm around my shoulder. "Will the child's father be in your life? Is there anything I can do to support you?"

I blew past her questions. "Can I take another test?"

Shaking her head, she got up, reached for the door, and motioned for me to follow. Back in the bathroom for the second time, I took a moment to look up at the sky, asking for God's mercy without words. I was in trouble.

"It's positive again," she said, now holding both tests.

I slid off the couch as panic set in. I wasn't just in trouble—I was screwed!

The lady showed me a diagram of a baby nestled in its mother's womb. "Based on your last period, your due date will be sometime late May next year. Wait, your baby looks more like this now," she said, showing me a different diagram.

I could still hear her muffled voice as the room began spinning around me counterclockwise. I wasn't trying to hear what she had to say and started scanning the room for the exit. I had to get out of there before she ruined what remained of my now-short life.

Sensing my despair, she asked again, "Is there anything I can do for you?"

Staring her dead in the face, I shook my head no. I now needed a place to stay, a job, and a car. How was she going to help me get those things?

"My mom is going to kill me." My mild sobs transitioned into torrential rainfall pouring from my eyes.

"I can call your mom and talk to her for you."

That was the last straw; I was truly convinced that this woman was nuts. I had to get out of there.

"My mother knows that I don't have a grown woman friend named Susan. And just so you know, she will kill us both," I shouted as I moved for the door. "Please don't call me or my house."

As I stepped out of the clinic, the cool air bit at my skin, each breath heavy with the weight of unspoken words. The path stretched before me, lined with trees that whispered secrets, yet all I could think about was the impending storm waiting at home.

With each step, my heart raced, thoughts spiraling like leaves caught in a gust. *Should I tell her when she first walked in, or wait until she was in bed?* My stomach twisted, a tight knot of uncertainty. Maybe I should talk to someone else and get their advice. *Nah. This was my decision to make, right?* Abortion never crossed my mind as a possible choice.

I just needed to think through my plan to break the news.

By the time my mom walked through the door, my fingers were twitching uncontrollably, a chill creeping up my spine as if the shadows in the room were whispering warnings. I did my best to stay out of her way, scanning her words and body language. I wanted to see if I could gauge her mood and find the perfect moment to tell her I had ruined my life. She'd slap me, and that would be the end. I could live to die another day.

Call me Chicken Little, because the perfect time never came, and my mom went to bed before I could give her the news. I entered her dark room for the first time, planning to just say the words "I'm pregnant" and wait for her reaction. Instead, I ended up going into her room and pretending I needed something off the dresser. I repeated this foolishness two more times before my mom sat up in bed, clearly annoyed by my erratic behavior.

"What in the hell is going on? Do you need something?" she asked. Even in the dim light, her gaze felt like ice, slicing through the quietness and wrapping around my throat, leaving me breathless and exposed.

"I'm, I'm...," I stammered.

"You are what?" she quickly responded to my half-formed thought.

"Pregnant."

As she turned, irritation flickered across her face, her voice a sharp knife cutting through my resolve to stay composed.

"Turn on the light so I can see how stupid you look."

Numb to her words, I turned on the light and should've ran then. The room felt cooler, maybe because cold water from the "shame bucket" had been dumped right over my head. I was soaking wet and unable to move.

I could feel her looking directly at me through my closed eyes. I couldn't bear to look at her—couldn't stomach the disappointment I would see and already felt. Doing so had the propensity to break me in two.

The shame transitioned into a blue whale devouring me in one gulp.

Unable to hold myself together, tears began flowing down my face. There was no prep that could've ever gotten me ready for this experience.

"What am I going to tell my friends?" she yelled at the top of her lungs.

I didn't return a response; there were no words or answers to give. The plan was to tell her the bad news and leave.

She continued to ramble on. "Do you know how to take care of a baby? Who is the baby daddy anyway?" She capitalized on my silence and continued with her rant, "You are getting an abortion. That's it. Now close my door; I have to go to work tomorrow."

I stepped back, the heaviness of her words crashing down. Shutting the door behind me felt like sealing away a part of my soul, and I fled to my room, my heart pounding in a frantic rhythm against my chest.

Sharing the news with my mom the next morning about my decision not to have an abortion set me up for a three-week silent treatment. If there were other people in the room when she walked in from work, she made it a point to ignore my being and call out their names as she greeted them. Her voice rang with warmth for everyone but me. There was no eye contact or mention of my existence. I was crushed.

Hearing her tell my aunts and friends about the pregnancy during her many phone calls hurt me even more. "What's she gonna do with a baby? I am not taking care of a baby. I won't do it!" Her declarations and tirades seemed nonstop. Her disgust with me hung in the air, heavy on my shoulders, shrinking my confidence by the day.

Calling my dad didn't bring any relief. "Dad, I need to tell you something," I said softly, my voice shaky. I wasn't ready to make the call, but my mom insisted that he hear the news from me before other family members revealed it.

His voice crackled over the line, hurried and clipped, as if he were fighting against the clock. "Yeah, Punkin, what is it? I'm working."

As soon as the word pregnant fell from my mouth, he cut me off. "Say what now? I knew I shouldn't have left. If I had still been there, this would have never happened. I told your mother about you and those boys. She didn't believe me about you."

I wasn't surprised one bit about him not being happy about what I had to say, but I had no idea he would make it about how his presence would have made all the difference.

In my heart, I knew God wasn't pleased with me either. In an attempt to give an offering, I remained quiet and gave my mom space during those lonely three weeks. I felt as if I had draped myself in a heavy shroud, the fabric woven with threads of shame and guilt, each step weighed down by her silent, but roaring, judgment.

This was not supposed to be me. At least that's what many of my elders said after learning that I was campaigning to be another statistic. It wasn't until one of my aunts thought I had suffered enough that she called my mother and told her to bury the hatchet, and she acquiesced.

"No more babies," my mom said firmly as she pulled me in for a hug. Relief swept over me, pulling me away from the tension that had plagued my heart, leaving no space for questions.

Before getting pregnant, I had big plans of going away to college and being rich by twenty-five. Now, I was destined to be a single teen mom working a minimum-wage job, living under my mom's thumb, and attending a local junior college. I finished high school early and increased my work hours to full-time in the kids clothing department at Sears and Roebuck. I had plans of making money and then taking some time off to look after the baby.

JD was born in May of 1998 during *The Oprah Winfrey Show* at a Catholic hospital on the north side of town. He came into this world three days before what would have been my senior prom and twenty-two days shy of my graduation ceremony.

Leading up to his birth, my body had grown weary as it prepared to take on the feat of moving life from inside me into my arms. My neck and lower back ached. I found it harder and harder to walk the three flights up to the apartment without pausing for a breathing break. My fingers started looking like smoked wieners as they expanded outward. I had never paid this much attention to the side effects of pregnancy before. I dreamt of the day when I would have my body back.

The few books I had read during my pregnancy talked about the importance of breathing and laboring at home as much as possible before going to the hospital. Given this guidance, I, too, had decided that this would be my plan once the contractions kicked in. I would, as the lady in the book suggested, breathe slowly through the pains and stay calm until that magical time arrived to head to the hospital.

The night before JD was to make his appearance, I felt a sharp pinch in both sides of my belly that came and went for at least two hours before picking up in intensity. "Ma! I think I'm in labor. I'm scared," I said, looking at my mom with the panic of a doe that knows she is about to be eaten by a pride of lions.

The books did a solid job describing what the pains would feel like, but they failed to mention the knife-like stabbing sensation slicing my ribs into shreds. The breathing techniques I hadn't practiced at all were not providing much comfort either.

"Please go get Auntie; I need some help if we are going to stay here longer." I had already called my childhood friend, Kia, to be with me while my mom drove to get Auntie. We had everything planned out.

As soon as my mom walked out the door, the agony kicked in tenfold, and I started screaming at the top of my lungs. "Shit! I can't take this!" The screaming seemed to energize the contractions, making them hurt even more. However, there was no turning back, as the dread kicked into full gear without mercy. "I'm outta here; carry me down the stairs," I pleaded with Kia.

Poor Kia tried to calm me down, "Friend, you have to stop screaming. Here, sit down. Your mom will be home soon."

She was lying. I didn't have to stop screaming. What would really happen if I did? Also, she didn't know when my mom would be home.

I wobbled from the couch, which had grown too hot for my tense body that had morphed into an ironing board, every muscle tensing in concert. I slid my feet into my worn flip-flops and started walking toward the kitchen, out the back door, and onto the porch. Tears began pouring down one by one.

This was not the labor I had envisioned. I was truly in over my head with this laboring experience, and this was only the beginning. By the time my mom returned,

I had started making my way down the many stairs, ignoring Kia's attempts to get me to wait before I fell.

My mom sped through all the lights that tried to get in her way. The song *Let's Chill* blasted over the radio, and I was scream-crying the lyrics, hoping to distract myself from what my body was engineered to do.

Anxiety had run away with my labor pains, turning me into a wreck in the process. Fear-filled thoughts raced through my mind. *You can't do this. This is what you get. You couldn't even stay home and breathe. How will you take care of a baby?*

Doubt began to settle in my brain, oozing down my face, neck, and the rest of my body. That's it; I would need to give in and ask for meds as soon as we got to the hospital. *What would I do if it was too late to get meds?*

Various scenarios played tennis in my head. I barely noticed that my mom pulled into the area where the ambulances arrived. She helped get me out of her car and into the hands of capable doctors. I could see in her eyes that she, too, had become concerned for me. Maybe she knew her baby wasn't ready to have a baby for real. And yet, here we were.

Once in the labor room, they placed the epidural, and I mostly slept and ate ice chips. Doctors and nurses cycled in and out of the room, doing things to my body and checking when I could start pushing. Twelve hours later, it was time.

"Push!" they instructed repeatedly.

I had no idea what that meant in my body.

"Bear down like you are taking a bowel movement," the doctor said.

I didn't know what it meant to push a baby out of my vagina. Who knows how to do that for real? I knew how to take a shit, but I couldn't feel anything down there because I was numb. I pushed for nearly forty minutes before my baby was pulled from my vaginal canal with forceps clamped to either side of his little head. My body had gone as far as it could; exhaustion had taken over.

Hearing his scream was startling at first. I mean, I knew there was a baby inside me that moved around, but it wasn't until I heard the shrill of his voice that I felt like this could be my new reality.

JD was placed into my arms, still crying. His olive-pale skin had been wiped somewhat clean of the slimy goo that covered his body. Wrapped tight in a white hospital blanket and snugly in my arms, I stared at his face intently, cracking a smile as I scanned his squinted almond-shaped eyes, perfectly round mouth, and colorless tears streaming down his tiny face.

He had a handful of dark, sleek strands covering his oddly shaped dome. Those forceps had smashed the sides of his head and caused me to worry that this oblong shape would last forever.

Several minutes passed before he calmed and settled into my embrace. Stillness came over the room. All of the chatter from the doctors, my mom, Kia, and others disappeared into the background.

It was just the two of us. I meticulously counted his fingers before pulling back the blanket to do the same with his toes. My eyes moved slowly from his feet to his belly and then to his barely visible neck, his pointy chin slightly concealing my view.

My gaze settled on his face, and our eyes met for the first time. His large, black-dotted pupils looked directly into mine. I pulled him closer to my heart as it melted like a stick of salted butter. I was his mommy now. I could hardly believe it.

CHAPTER 7:

London Bridges

I started my college career at a local junior college three months after I gave birth to JD. While I was still pregnant, my mom had agreed to care for him while I attended classes. Her job of twelve years was phasing out, and instead of taking the gig they offered, she ran out the door with a severance package in hand. This timing ended up being perfect; her newfound freedom gave her space to take me to my doctor's appointments and start new hobbies.

My mom began dating again and joined a class for steppers, where she met new friends and partied a few days a week. I hated it. I hated helping her pick which shoes would match her tiny dress. She'd twirl her skinny body around so I could fully see her outfit before deciding. Despite all of her hobbies, she kept her promise to watch the baby through my first year, or until I was able to secure another sitter who could meet her standards.

JD was such a sweet baby. He enjoyed being close to me at all times, cooing at the sight of my face and often returning my smile. I quickly learned that even a sweet baby needed a mom who knew how to step up her game when bedtime rolled around. There were nights when JD and I were wailing in unison—my last resort when my luck had run short and exhaustion had won by a landslide.

My mother, true to her word of not raising a baby, did not intervene. She never came riding in on a unicorn with a cape to save the day. Not one time.

My lack of parental experience ultimately wore down my patience and confidence, leading me to doubt whether I could actually be any good. Before becoming JD's mom, I had only babysat a handful of little ones for a few hours at most. I knew the basics— how to change a diaper, feed and burp a baby, and play with them. However, I never learned how to properly bathe a baby or soothe them when they weren't feeling well. I found babysitting to be fun, but the thrill was handing them back when my shift ended.

JD ended up spending every night of his first six months sleeping on my chest. He would wake up whenever I moved an inch in an attempt to transfer him to the bed. On the rare occasion that I could make it past that first step, he'd startle awake when his little body was lowered down toward the crib. Consequently, the crib involuntarily transitioned into a filled-to-the-brim clean clothes hamper.

My life was consumed with my studies and with being JD's mom. I had decided to take general education courses because I no longer knew what I wanted to be when I grew up, and I was so bored with school. My friends were living out my fairytale while I sat on the sidelines. This wasn't the college experience I had dreamed about.

My friendship with Kia fizzled as we both outgrew each other's bullshit. The disagreements reached a point of no return or resolve, causing distance to set in. The struggle to identify with her needs felt like a lift well beyond my reach and interest. So, I gave up.

Even though that relationship came to a slow and painful close, others continued to evolve despite their fair share of ups and downs. We were always able to make our way back to each other and not let conflict get the best of what we were trying to build through our connection.

My friendship with Chantel, a friend I met in high school, was able to face the wind without sinking the ship. Her blunt communication, tough love, and tendency to show up during the hard times are the things that I love most about her. It was also what I missed when she moved away to attend college too many miles away. She did her best with sending letters detailing the fun, new friends, and parties that come along with college experiences. I relished how she was able to live life on her terms without the responsibility of caring for another human.

Now, don't get me wrong. I definitely did my fair share of kicking it whenever I could get my hands on a babysitter and an ID that allowed me to access the really good parties. I targeted the parties where both the older men and the alcohol were plentiful, places where I could find new ways to complicate my life and cry about it later.

By the time I was twenty-one, I was bitter and insecure about how I presented myself to the world. Intuitively, I felt out of place and unsure of myself. When people saw me, they saw JD and me. I was now a package deal and struggling to accept it.

My aunts and other family members did their best to soothe my wounds with praises for being a good mom and staying on track with my studies. They didn't know too many girls who would still pursue their dreams after having a baby at such a young age. "Most girls would have just given up," they said.

To them, I was still living the dream. To me, I was living in my version of hell. Going to school felt like a waste of time; I was making nine dollars an hour as a law clerk and attracting fools left and right. Every time I mentioned being a mom, a storm of questions rained down on me, each one feeling like a sharp jab. "So, where is your baby daddy? Are y'all still together?"

"Well, I mean we were never together," was my canned reply. "He's around, but just for JD."

I suppose that was mostly true. Kiren would pop in and out of JD's life, but not with the consistency I had hoped for. He, too, seemed to be living life like my friends. Becoming a parent had kicked his previously-forgotten college plans into motion. He moved on campus at a local university and carried on as if he had not accepted full responsibility for the life he had created.

Sometimes our calls would end with my pleas for financial help; other times, my voice would fall silent while he berated me and minimized my agony. "I'm doing the best I can. Did you call my parents? Maybe they can do something. I mean, what do you want me to fucking do?"

Contempt for Kiren festered in my chest, a bitter seed that took root, growing deep and twisted like the weeds in my neglected garden. These feelings overstayed their invitation and proved far more virulent than the resentment I felt while helping my mom pick out her club clothes.

I spent countless hours in my twenties pouring

my heart out in a journal—detailing my challenges, pleading with God to help, and making promises to myself to be different, only to break them later. An emptiness gnawed at my insides, a hollow echo that left me shivering in a crowded room, desperately seeking warmth in the smiles of others. Life was happening to me, and I had given in to the fact that I wasn't the active participant that I wanted to be.

What happened to my sense of self? I would ask God. Why is it that I had been lying on my fucking back and watching unimaginable things happen? I had lost all my fire and believed that everyone else knew it, confirmed by the way they treated me. I wanted my fire back. I wanted it all back—my dignity, my purpose.

So, I made plans to take back my control through self-discipline. No more laying down for others, period. No more letting snide comments roll off my shoulders or allowing malicious behaviors to occur at my expense. I was hopeful that one day things would pick up for me. I just didn't know when.

Years would slip by like grains of salt through my fingers before I would finally confront the truth of my choices—but not before I aborted the second baby that made its way into my uterus.

Anxiety twisted in my stomach as I counted the days since my last period. JD hadn't even turned one. This time was different from the first. I had been consistently on my condom game, even turning down sex with partners who didn't want to wear one.

The thought of being pregnant again sent my mind racing with fear. *How could I let this happen again?* I was going to let everyone down—even myself. What about the plea deal I had made with my mom? No more babies. She would probably turn her back and withdraw her support if I turned up pregnant again.

Parenting was already hard as hell. I barely knew how to survive taking care of one baby. How in the hell could I manage two? Again, my denial told me there was no way I could be pregnant. And yet, the pregnancy test came back positive. There was no need to take a second one this time. Staring at the two pink lines brought beads of ice cold sweat on my temples. How had I let this happen once more?

Racking my brain, I recalled a drunken night after the club when I had sex with a college classmate. There was a condom in place when we started and also a weird pause when his hands were not visible to me. It dawned on me, as I sat in the bathroom staring at the positive test, that the condom had either broken or been removed without my consent.

Either way, I hadn't signed up for this outcome.

There was only one choice—no consulting with others or weighing options. With trembling hands, I called the clinic the next morning.

My bank account fell short of covering the option that included general anesthesia. However, I was still firm on moving forward. No more babies. Now, I just had to hold on to my secret for the next two weeks until I could get this taken care of.

The night before my abortion was hectic. I tossed and turned, plagued by awful thoughts about all the things that could go wrong. *What if I died? What if they couldn't get the baby out and I had to give birth anyway? Did I really need to do this? Was I making a big mistake that I wouldn't be able to take back?*

I lay awake for the last two hours before it was time to get up. I would need to take three buses to my destination. My nerves got the best of me as I turned on the shower, and my eyes began to leak. I couldn't do this by myself.

"Ma, I gotta tell you something. Please listen," I said, walking into her bedroom where she had just gotten up.

"I'm pregnant, but I don't want to keep the baby. I know that I can't handle another baby. I made an appointment. It's today. I need your help. Can you go with me?"

She tilted her head to the side before saying, "What time is the appointment? Go get dressed." She didn't seem mad at all. There were no questions about how this happened or who the baby's father was.

Her reaction stunned me momentarily, but I shook it off. I had minimal energy to expend on my usual mental gymnastics. Instead, I heeded her directions and got dressed so we could head out. The sooner I could get this taken care of, the sooner it could all be behind me, behind us.

The clinic was on the north side, about forty minutes from our apartment in morning, rush-hour traffic. The car ride there was silent, only the radio interrupting the quiet from time to time.

Pulling up to the shabby storefront facility made what I was about to do feel real. As we walked in and approached the counter, I could feel the cold stares from the many girls who, like me, had come to abort their babies. Unbothered by the environment, my mother stood next to me as I checked in before deciding to step in front of me to take over. I was relieved, only chiming in when needed.

"When was your last period?" the lady asked. Based on my response, I was eight weeks pregnant, which meant that my procedure price, without the local anesthesia, would be in the lowest tier.

My mother jumped at the thought of me being awake. "She has to go under. What is the price for the extra medication?" my mom said matter-of-factly.

Turning to look at me, she insisted, "You need to go under." I was grateful for her being with me. What would have happened had I not told her?

We settled into the first waiting room. Finally, a lady opened a wooden door across the way. "Number seven-ty-two," she called. It was time for me to go back.

My knees cracked as I stood. There was a long walk down the dimly lit hallway on the other side of the door. The dingy white linoleum tile floor squeaked under my sneakers.

After changing into the hospital gown, I was told to sit in yet another waiting room. This time the room was filled with girls one step closer to their procedures too. I could barely hold my head up, too embarrassed to make eye contact. I spent my time locking eyes with my feet and half-listening to whatever daytime TV show was playing.

Some of the girls were making small talk with each other. I wanted to engage and ask questions but lacked the courage to voice them. Hours passed with me in that room, without a single word passing from my lips.

They said I would only be here four to six hours, but at this rate, I wouldn't be home until the evening. Why was time moving quickly on the clock but crawling like molasses in my body? The wait gave me more time to negotiate and make promises to myself.

You can't do this again. This doesn't fix things. You need to be more careful. There's still time to get things right. No more messing around. Focus on your studies and the baby you already have. This will be the last time.

I kept repeating that last promise over and over. When it was finally my turn, I shuffled back to a sterile, cold table. The chill of the metal seeped into my skin. My mind was a haze, the muffled countdown of "ten, nine, eight..." echoing like a distant memory as darkness pulled me into a deep sleep.

The next thing I remember, I was hearing a nurse's voice, "You did great. You have another hour before you can leave." Her words crashed into me like a gentle wave. I glanced around the recovery room, seeing the other girls laying in their beds, each of us bound by a choice that felt both unthinkable and necessary.

My mind started racing again with questions. *Were there other roads we could have taken? What led us all here?* For me, I could almost hear the echoes of judgment from friends and family. The thought of another baby daddy, another broken promise.

The car ride home was quiet and calm. Still woozy from the anesthesia, I was relieved to lay down in the reclined seat that my mom helped to prepare. There was some music playing from the nearly turned-off radio, just enough to send me back to sleep. By the time I woke up, we had pulled back up to our house and JD was patiently waiting for me to notice him nestled in his car seat. I had conveniently slept right through his pickup from a family member's house.

That evening, I kept my Red Lobster dinner plans with friends. I felt fine. The cramps the nurse said would bother me for the next couple of days never came. The whole situation was easier than I had ever imagined it would be. I dodged a major bullet.

In my heart, I felt like I could pick up my life where

I'd left off before this happened. This day would mark the last time I talked about my first abortion.

CHAPTER 8:

Sticks and Stones

I was now twenty-three, and Stephen and I had been dating for about six months. I felt somewhat able to balance the demands of being JD's mom, my college studies, and part-time work duties as a bank teller. And, so far, having a boyfriend was working out too.

Our time together was spontaneous and filled mostly with laughter when it was just the two of us. There were times when he would become really angry and say some pretty messed-up things to me. Easily agitated, his light-switch behavior reminded me a lot of my dad.

"You think you're better than me...than other people. Do you think I'm ugly?" Stephen would ask.

I never responded. Knowing the limitless sharpness of my tongue, no good could come. Plus, I'd fully taken stock of his appearance when we met and accepted that, while his physical attributes weren't my usual type, he had all the other qualities that helped to make him a fit.

He was 5'3" at best, with dark, bluish-black skin. His face had two oval-shaped eye sockets with dark brown pupils surrounded by a yellow tint. His large, bright pink lips disappeared when his crowded, yellow-streaked teeth peeked through. Stephen mostly wore his hair in braids that were either half done or overdue for a refresh. It was as if he only half-cared about his image or what others thought of it.

He liked nice things, had his own place and car, and didn't cling to his money. He was a drug dealer who loved to spend money on me, even though he had two young sons. Because of his profession, his communication was inconsistent, the days were long, and nights of being alone were plentiful. This sporadic frequency allowed me the freedom to easily weave lies together. The arrangement worked well for us.

The only hitch was the hateful words that came spewing from his mouth. Most times, I would ignore him, which I think only angered him more, but didn't change my approach. Whenever I was in the mood to placate him, I'd carefully dismiss his claims and deescalate the situation.

Early into our courtship, I started to get the feeling that he unknowingly hated himself and me. Unfortunately, this realization didn't outweigh the benefits of keeping him around. I had grown accustomed to the mistreatment that came and went.

Transactional relationships with selfish men were all I knew. Kiren was also good at cursing me out when my behavior didn't align with whatever he wanted at the time. I had accepted that relationships were just hard, and this one with Stephen was no different.

I wasn't alone. My friends were dealing with similar bullshit—the numerous lies, other women, and the infamous breakup-to-makeup cycle that my favorite music artists sang so passionately about. What

I was experiencing felt normal; there was no reason to question this truth.

The night things changed for me started off like any other. Stephen and I went out to dinner and had several drinks. JD was away with his dad for the weekend, so we had made plans to stay overnight at a nearby hotel.

The door barely closed before his hands were on me, tugging at my clothes and pushing me toward the bed. Something had triggered him somewhere between exiting the car and entering the hotel elevator. I had never felt unsafe with him before. His eyes bulged from their sockets as he intently unbuttoned my jeans.

"We are going to make a baby tonight, and you are going to keep it," he said, giving me a death stare.

The anger in his eyes felt misplaced; this was someone I had slept with several times before. Tonight would not have been any different had he not transformed into a saber-toothed dragon trying to eat me alive.

"Stephen! Stephen, what are you doing?" I tried to get his attention, hoping he would snap out of this trance if he could see what he was doing to me.

We wrestled a bit, him ending up on top of me. My strength was fading, and I felt my muscles giving way. My arms, once raised in the air, were now pinned above my head on the bed. He stripped off both my panties and my pants in one swift motion.

By this time, I had started screaming bloody murder, and panic had taken over. I was in danger and did my best to fight back, but it wasn't enough to stop him from pushing himself inside, each thrust sending a rug burn sensation through my vaginal walls and into my clenched throat.

The room fell into complete silence. My soul left

my body and hovered above to observe the tragedy. I saw myself lying there, lifeless and helpless. I thought about all my mom's warnings when I was younger, about what happens when you go to the second location. This couldn't have been what she was talking about. I knew this man; I even cared about him.

My senses went into withdrawal. With my eyes closed, I could hear murmurs of words coming from Stephen, but I couldn't make them out. The pain, disguised as heat, that was moving through my body had started to dull. My arms remained pinned until he finished.

It was only after he removed his sweaty body from mine that I could feel the tears trickling down the sides of my face. I laid there in complete shock, unable to wrap my head around what had just happened. I did the only thing I could and rolled into a fetal position with my back to Stephen, who had fallen asleep, and remained there until morning came.

The car ride home was quiet. I had no words; the contents of my brain had been emptied. My shame cloak had doubled in size during the past several hours, becoming large enough to boast a hood that could also cover my eyes. It felt like a source of protection from the stares and snide comments of those who disapproved of my choices.

Before getting out of that car with Stephen, what resembled regret came across his face. I slammed his door, trying to break the fucking window. The cloak had magical powers too, helping me to easily access anger and scorch the earth without blinking twice.

After that night, I made it a point to refuse many, but not all, of his requests to see one another again. There would be no more hotel hangouts or going to his house, but my codependence kept me entangled with him. Each time I saw him, I thought about that horrible night, but we never talked about it. We never called it what it was—rape.

It turns out he had gotten exactly what he wanted. His heinous act had resulted in a baby trying to grow in my womb. Watching my urine inch across the pregnancy stick was pointless. I already knew the result in my heart, as well as the plan to have an abortion. So, when the second dark line showed up, my next move was making the call for abortion money.

"Stephen, I'm pregnant," I said to him over the phone. My face was hot. The other end of the line was quiet. I could only hear the music coming through his car speakers. "Do you hear me?" I screamed out of desperation.

"So why are you telling me? What do you want me to do?" His response felt like a bee sting to the eye. What in the hell was he talking about? This was all his doing, and now he was pretending otherwise.

I screamed through the phone, "I'm not keeping this baby. I don't want any more kids. I told you that!"

Stephen hung up on me almost immediately, and I moved forward with scheduling the appointment that would take place in two short weeks. I was broke as a joke, with plenty of bills to pay. I calculated in my mind which ones I could not pay in order to cover the $300. I didn't feel comfortable asking anyone else. The only answer was that Stephen had to pay for the mistake he made, and I'd be the one to ensure that he did.

The clinic wasn't the only call I made that day. I reached out to anyone and everyone who would listen to my sob story of being pregnant and having an abortion.

"I'm so fucking mad at his ass," I would say, intentionally leaving out the hotel part of the story.

"Girl, so what did he say? Is he going to help pay?" was the common response.

"Are you sure you want to have another abortion? You know you can't keep having abortions," were the sentiments coming from others.

They were right, and so was I. Having a baby and caring for a child that was a product of rape wasn't the plan for me. *Could I ever be capable of loving this child or another child at all? And, oh, what would my mom say? What about my aunts? I was already on the path to making my life right after having JD; could I really do that again? Could I do it again with or without the dad being there?*

I had also started to feel a loathing toward Stephen taking root in my heart. There was no way that this could work. This was my only option. I would repeat those words to myself over and over.

Stephen ghosted me on the first day of a two-day procedure. I called him at least a hundred times. Sometimes he would answer just to yell, "Stop calling my phone, bitch!" or use other foul words.

I held zero regard for his feelings; I just needed the cash. "Just give me the money, and I will go away. I am NOT having your baby!"

I was determined to not let his voice, thick with anger, drown out my resolve. His money to cover the procedure never came, but my determination to abort the child ultimately won.

This time, I opted for an at-home abortion. I didn't want to sit in the clinic for what felt like fifty-eleven million hours, surrounded by those girls talking. I craved the quiet of my friend's place, drowning out the world. I imagined curling up on her bed and the only witnesses being trusted sources.

I mean, how bad could it be? I'd heard that this type of abortion wasn't painful. I'd already survived birth, and those contractions were awful. I definitely could do this.

After inserting the suppository in place, I drove to my friend's house to rest and wait things out. She couldn't open the door fast enough. My body twisted in discomfort and agony under the burden of relentless cramps.

Hours passed. Moaning in unison with the pain provided brief solace. After a few rounds of vomiting bile, I sat perched on the edge of the toilet as sweat slowly started excreting from my scalp. Suddenly, a slick warmth slipped away, disappearing in the water below. What followed was a tranquilizing silence and wave of relief.

CHAPTER 9:

Hey Love

My mid-twenties—the two to three years before I met Cliff—literally flew by before my eyes. I started and finished grad school. I also continued the pattern of brief entanglements with men without any real love connection, often finding myself in one-way love situations.

I suffered the loss of several loved ones, including my maternal grandmother, a grandmother figure, and a dear friend's father, who had become a surrogate dad to me. These deaths, coupled with my financial struggles, gnawed at my spirit and kept me up at night. On the surface, I was trying to provide JD and myself with everything I thought we needed and wanted, but all I got was mounting debt and stress.

The walls I built to protect the fort from another attack grew higher and stronger, causing greater disconnection.

Decade-long friendships were strained by my withdrawal and erratic displays of fiery emotion, often brought on by the many ways I'd been wronged. Only a handful of friendships survived this period and emerged stronger. The others became distant memories—carcasses that got buried along with the secrets.

I journaled heavily during these times as a means to purge and process my experiences. Documenting my feelings and wishes for a brighter tomorrow gave me some hope. I felt desperate to let go of the heavy past in order to make room for a lighter future. Countless entries spoke of a process that began with understanding what had happened, followed by an aspiration for acceptance so that I could let go and be free.

Back then, letting go hindered my progress. It sounded like forgiveness, a concept that felt elusive and perhaps, tied to my ability to forgive myself. Even though I was caught in a cycle without the ability to see options, I was curious about what could be at the root of my troubles.

I pondered in my journal:

I used to think I was "good" at forgiving when, in fact, I realize that I had only mastered the skill of minimizing the "wrong" and moving on without truly forgetting or acknowledging my involvement. Ironically, I thought I had demonstrated forgiveness with my dad and Kiren, but the truth is that I had numbed myself just enough to protect me until I was faced with dealing with each of them.

It all rests on me and my inability to move on. Life continuously presents reminders of how difficult it is for me to forgive, forget, and move forward. I don't know how to progress—not in this life. I haven't mastered this. I have a tendency to hold onto the past, leaving me stuck in it. This burden is so crippling that it feels like a sin. I wonder if my unwillingness

*to forgive is connected to my ability to forgive myself.
Maybe.*

Stumped by what my next steps should look like, I ended these entries with pleas to God to fix my situation. I begged for guidance, hope, faith, or some other synonym capable of alleviating the pressure in my chest that felt ready to burst at any moment.

My last relationship before meeting Cliff turned out to be another short-lived, volatile connection with a guy I met in a dark club. We argued about every-thing—from where we would eat dinner to why he hadn't answered my countless calls. There was never resolution between us. He'd just find ways to pacify me until the next hiccup arose.

His past was a mystery. He would occasionally say things that gave me a glimpse into who he was before we met. I dismissed his omissions because I, too, held secrets. "I had a son who died a while ago; I hate his mother for making me agree to the eye surgery," he randomly said one night when I asked about his children.

We were together for a little over a year before I grew tired of the strain and having to explain why we were together to friends and family. I lacked the words to justify our connection, one of many signs that I needed to end the relationship.

It wasn't lost on me that my sense of self had also fallen by the wayside. In my relentless pursuit to understand him and identify the "thing" that was holding our relationship together, I had completely disassociated from myself.

I walked away looking for the fast-forward button. I needed that relationship to be in the rearview mirror, a forgettable blur as I sped in the other direction. A part of me felt the relief of letting go, while other parts felt conflicted. Fear had made itself at home in my heart, and it was in a full-on war with my desires to move forward. The regret from my past decisions was weighing me down, and I didn't know how to move on.

After much reflection, I realized that this relationship had taught me two of the biggest lessons in life. First, I saw how important it is to allow others to be who they are while being mindful of who I am too. And second, when it's "right" between you and your person, you will be at your best. Your partner will be able to embrace your best self and encourage you to be just that.

The plan was to give myself some time to just be. I was in a space of questioning how to get back to doing things that could help me return to the path of living a purposeful life. I had no idea what my purpose was but knew that what I was experiencing wasn't it. It couldn't be.

For the second time in my life, I was confused about what I wanted to do professionally. I questioned my motivations for wanting to be in a relationship and wondered whether I could be patient and wait for God to bring the right person into my life, or if I could be happy with myself while I waited.

I felt internally weak, as if I could break and fold at any moment. The feeling of giving up scared me but also seemed like a viable option. I had grown impatient with trying to improve my quality of life and felt unable to move forward or succeed in something worthwhile. Even in parenthood, I felt like I wasn't living up to the expectations I had set for myself.

As fate would have it, I gave myself little to no time to process my past and the emotions that ruled my behaviors. Something shiny and new captured my time and attention. I met Cliff on a blind date a month after ending my last relationship. My friend, responsible for the setup, was convinced that he was the one for me. She had been introduced to him while on a date with one of his childhood friends. "Girl, I met the perfect guy for you. His name is Cliff. I even got his phone number for you," she said, excitement bubbling in her voice.

I wasn't convinced by her enthusiasm, and I brushed it off. I never took the number. I mean, what kind of guy would expect me to make the first call? Nah, he couldn't be the one.

A month passed before Cici called, insisting that I get dressed to hang out. "Tonight is the night; you are going to meet Cliff. Trust me, friend, you are going to like him," she said. "Worst comes to worst, you'll get a free meal out of the deal," she added with a chuckle.

She was right; I did like free food. Plus, curiosity began to creep in, urging me to see this guy that my friend had been so sure about. I took her up on the offer and decided to get dressed up in fitted jeans, a white bodysuit, a cropped black jacket with cute eyelets, and comfy platform heels. At the very least, I could make a strong first impression and look good while doing it.

My excitement immediately started to wane when we pulled up to our destination, which was not a restaurant, but was instead someone's house. "That's him," she said, pointing at a guy sitting on the trunk of a car, wearing a white T-shirt, jeans, and sneakers. Cliff was in no way dressed properly to go on a date with a girl like me. I noticed that he was smoking, and judgment squarely entered the room.

"Oh girl, we should leave now. I don't like smokers." In my head, this was a deal breaker, and the date was over—until she turned off the car and proceeded to get out. Shit.

As I walked across the street and Cliff 's image came into full view, my doubt shifted to intrigue. This man was striking. He kept the cigar in his mouth as he shook my hand, while my friend continued to ramble about whatever. His hands were soft and warm, like his butterscotch skin. My breath paused when a smile appeared on his face, revealing a thin gap between his two front teeth, serving as a sweet compliment to the manicured goatee that framed his mouth.

Cliff was a man of few words at dinner, recovering from a hangover from the night before. I watched his mouth move whenever the rare word came up and out. The attraction I felt for him was so instant that I failed to notice it was unrequited at that point.

As the night progressed, Cliff opened up about his plans to play *Scrabble* with his bedridden grandmother. He said he needed to leave early to settle the score with her. As someone who had lost two grandmothers the previous year, my heart did backflips at hearing about their relationship. *Scrabble* was also a game I played with ease and had many victories under my belt. The spark between us had been ignited.

Cliff called me late that night after a win against his grandmother, and we talked about anything and everything until the wee hours of the morning. I learned that he was a successful business owner, had attended Tennessee State University, had an older sister, and was the product of married parents. So much of his background fit into the picture I had drawn for an ideal partner.

The very next day after meeting, we not only went out to lunch together, but also had dinner at my place in the evening. We listened to deep R&B jams from present day and the nineties. I was impressed by his love of music and his freedom to belt out the lyrics as if he was standing on a stage in front of a huge crowd. He managed to sing me into a captivating trance, strong enough to give him the edge he needed to win our first-ever *Scrabble* match.

We spent every day after making and keeping plans to learn all that we could about each other. On what felt like the third date, Cliff asked whether I would be open to being a mom again. Prior to meeting him, I'd been having conversations with God and my mom about this very thing—coming to the realization that I loved being JD's mom but not the experience it took to get here. If the right person came along, I believed that having a do-over would do my heart some good.

"I know that I want to be a dad. I would be good at it too. If you said you didn't want to have any more kids, that would be a dealbreaker for me."

Never had I ever had a conversation with a man about having kids on purpose.

The light in my heart beamed brighter when he was around. This man asked me about my dreams and the type of life that I wanted to live when I got older. Equally important, he was interested in hearing about my plans for making my ideal future a reality. It was refreshing. I realized how consumed I'd been with surviving in the present day.

My mind would take me maybe a couple of years

into the future, but life had left me very little time to dream about tomorrow's operational plan.

I know it sounds crazy, but I realized a few weeks after meeting Cliff that he was my person. My mom smiled and shook her head in amazement when I shared that I wanted to marry him.

There was something so special about the pacing of our conversations and the endless hours we spent together. I never felt like I had to be anyone other than myself around him. We welcomed the stillness when together or on the phone, filling the space with ease. Our shared interests in music, food, and classic movies strengthened our bond. I couldn't get enough of him.

I loved his excitement about wanting to get to know JD and spend time with both of us. Those two connected in their shared interests in basketball and baseball and their love in making me smile. JD was also intrigued by Cliff's career path and how vastly different it was from how other adults in his life made money. Cliff was confident in his explanation of what he did on any given day, the money gained, and what was next to keep building his empire. He also exhibited patience and openness to the many questions thrown his way from an eager ten-year-old.

While I was impressed by Cliff's business acumen, that journey felt foreign and sounded too risky for a gal like me. I needed to know when my next dollar was coming and exactly how much it would be. I believed then, and even today, that the differences in our paths are the reason for the many new adventures we've shared together. It was these experiences that gave me peace about our potential to create a life that we both wanted.

Our view on marriage is where our paths diverged.

He believed that being married wouldn't change the quality of a relationship. To him, the societal pressures to get married weren't enough of a reason to do it. He was open to marriage "one day," but it wasn't a priority. He had seen too many people drift apart after jumping the broom.

For the twenty-eight-year-old me, marriage was a dream. Yes, marriage had escaped my mother, but that wouldn't be my fate. Getting married was the ultimate goal after finding and connecting with my person. Being a wife meant that I was no longer just a baby mama; it would show the world that I was capable of being one with another person, and the security I had longed for would finally be mine. I would be taken care of and have someone that I could count on to show up time and time again.

I didn't give much thought to our varying views on marriage. I figured that when the time came, we would know what to do. Instead, I leaned into my independently created fairytale and applied pressure to our circumstances to ensure alignment.

We faced challenges early in our courtship, with Cliff cutting off contact with me for days and weeks at a time while I chased him down. This pattern repeated until I gave him the ultimatum—he would lose me if he ever disappeared again.

I later learned that he was in love with me and that our connection was special to him, but it also scared him. He used that time away to focus on work and be alone with his thoughts. His explanation went in one ear and out the other; I just wanted to make sure that he was going to stay like he said he would.

The narrow focus on my needs made it easy to dismiss the impact of the real estate crash in 2008 that suddenly decimated everything Cliff had worked so hard to build. His finances were slowly draining along with his energy to maintain the image that he had built.

Before the crash, Cliff anticipated and answered my needs without me voicing them. This man brought groceries, cooked, and cleaned. We often joked about who could pull out their debit card the fastest when out shopping or going out to dinner. Most times, he was victorious, and that deepened my sense of security with him being in my life. So, when the financial troubles came, I remained convinced that they wouldn't last forever and blindly continued pushing for progress. By the end of our second year together, we were making plans to move in together and start a family.

CHAPTER 10:

Cinco Strong

"This baby is coming tonight!"

It was 2011, and I was lying in a hospital at twenty-four weeks pregnant trying to process what my obstetrician had just said. Her voice was low and shaky as she transitioned to the foot of the bed to check my cervix and confirm how many centimeters had given way. The severe pains from contractions had ceased, but the contents of the room started swirling as she continued to murmur words about what we could expect in the next several moments.

"We need to move quickly. You have a few options for the delivery. Would you like to have the baby vaginally or via C-section?" she asked. "The choice is yours, but it's important to know that the baby is very small, and a vaginal birth could result in a lot of tugging on the baby's body."

Time slowed. The words "C-section" and "vaginal birth" danced around my head before seeping slowly into my ears, one word at a time. My heart was beating a mile a minute, and I found it hard to grasp the reality that my baby would be here soon. My thoughts were racing like a morning train barreling out of the station.

With every word spoken, the train got further and further away from me.

It slowly dawned on me that both this train and a full-term pregnancy were out of my reach. The baby that I had only carried for twenty-four weeks would be making its debut today. Cliff and I had purposely held off on learning the baby's gender because we wanted to savor the surprise. This wasn't quite what we had in mind.

Brief pauses punctuated each of her words as the once-bright room started to grow dim. I felt like I was in a horror movie, holding Cliff 's hand in the engulfing darkness. A flashlight pierced the doctor's chin and radiated upward, her thin face eerily pale and decorated with two dark black dots that served as her windows to the world. Her gaze fixed upon us, Cliff and I kept turning our eyes to each other every few seconds, checking to make sure we were still in this together.

"So, what do you both want to do? Again, we don't have much time," urgency lacing her tone.

There was no time to consult each other before deciding. Without hesitation, we looked at one another and said, "Let's do a C-section."

The doctor let out an audible sigh of relief.

"I'm so glad you both chose this route. I am concerned about how small the baby will be, and we want to move as swiftly as possible."

As she was explaining the many risks associated with C-section procedures, she was interrupted by a notification from a pager tethered to her left hip. She promptly got up and left, her disappearance bringing a second sigh of relief, this time from us.

This couldn't be happening.

My brain started to replay the events of the day, trying to make sense of it all. I had woken up feeling not quite like myself but couldn't find the words to explain my symptoms. My mind was foggy, and there were tight squeezes traveling across the front of my belly. Different from contraction-like squeezes, they felt like unwarranted bear hugs that would last several seconds before dissipating.

Despite the odd sensations, I had still managed to make my way into work for a few hours. By late morning, I called Cliff to tell him that something wasn't right. He urged me to call the doctor for a same-day appointment. The OB we routinely saw wasn't in that day, but they said I could come in and see another doctor in the same practice.

It took me more than an hour to make the drive and walk into the office. By the time I arrived, the pain level had spiked considerably. After checking my cervix and confirming that it had opened by two centimeters, the doctor reassured me that this was normal.

"All is well; you are experiencing round ligament pains. We often see dilation happening early in second pregnancies," she said.

She was dismissive of my feelings and descriptions of the pains I felt in my body.

"Go home, take a warm bath, and rest," were her last, infamous words. While her confidence hadn't transferred onto me, I still decided to go home and follow her guidance.

Several hours passed, and the pain grew more intense with each second that went by. Ten minutes into my warm bath, I yelled for Cliff. I could barely move and needed help getting out of the tub. The pains, now feeling all too familiar, were definitely contractions. One after another, they came and went, like sharp knives digging into both sides of my belly. The bear hugs of earlier had morphed into a ten-foot boa constrictor tightening around my tense body. Fear crept into my heart; I knew something was terribly wrong.

Cliff raced us to the hospital. Five hours had passed since I'd left the appointment. Upon our arrival, the triage nurse informed us that my cervix had dilated to five centimeters, preparing my body for labor. It was at this point that they'd brought the doctor in to discuss our options.

I kissed Cliff goodbye before being rolled out of triage and into the operating room for the C-section. Once there, a nurse stood in front of me, holding my hands as a burning, cold rush of liquid numbed my lower half, the medicine taking hold as I was slowly lowered onto the cold table.

Blinding lights flickered overhead, illuminating a flurry of blurred bodies dancing in and out of my sight.

The anesthesiologist leaned over, "Do you feel that? Can you feel me touching your legs?"

I shook my head no.

Cliff was then guided in to sit at my bedside. I felt relieved by his presence and the warmth coming from his body onto the right side of my neck. His bloodshot eyes told the story of the anxiety swirling inside. His demeanor startled me; I hadn't seen him scared until now.

"Start now," uttered a distant voice.

With each passing minute, Cliff called my name until I responded with a weak, "Huh."

He would later tell me that I went in and out of consciousness, and he needed to ensure that I was still with him. This call-and-response ping pong continued until we heard a doctor say, "Hey baby. The time is 5:37 a.m."

Deafening silence fell over the room. There was no chatter, no sound of a screaming baby. The doctors' backs shielded our view as they rushed through the push door leading to the adjacent room. Why couldn't we see our baby? What were they hiding from us?

Panic started to rise again. I looked at Cliff, who responded with a tight squeeze to my right hand, providing what little reassurance he could. No words were spoken as we waited. Time moved at a snail's pace, and the once chatter-filled room had grown too quiet, lacking the peace one would expect from such silence.

Looking through the door window, we saw a doctor returning to the room. "The baby is fine and has been placed on a ventilator," she said. Her face showed relief, as if the hard part had been done.

We both jumped in with the million-dollar question. "Is it a boy or a girl?"

Unaware of the answer, she had to go back into the room to formulate her response.

"I will be right back."

A couple of months earlier, Cliff had abruptly awoken from a dream in which he envisioned the birth. His voice was calm. "It's a boy. It was just you and me. I saw it all," he said.

I had shaken my head in disbelief and drifted back to sleep. There was no way it could just be us alone. Both of our families were anxiously awaiting the birth and had already begun making plans about who would be there to witness it.

The doctor returned minutes later. "It's a boy."

I turned to look at Cliff, and we simultaneously shared a brief smile to celebrate the birth of our son. The gift of motherhood settled upon me once more — bittersweet joy, mingled with the fear of the unknown.

Some hours had passed since the delivery, and the time had come to move me from recovery into my room. On the way there, Cliff, along with a nurse, wheeled me through the large NICU doors leading to Cinco's incubator, which was surrounded by several machines. The white light inside the incubator highlighted his tiny body, covered with colorful wires. This was the child that we had prayed and waited for.

I immediately began counting his fingers and toes and noticed the black mask over his eyes, stopping short of his button nose and mouth. His miniature body was perfect in every way. I had never seen a baby this small; he weighed a mere pound and nine ounces. I was struck by how long his legs were; his measurements revealed that he was nineteen inches long.

I couldn't take my eyes off him, watching his chest move in harmony with the ventilator. As I gently reached toward the incubator, my fingers brushed against the cool, smooth surface of the black wrapping, hesitating for a moment before I pushed my hand into the incubator's warmth.

The moment our fingers touched, a spark ignited — a fragile and immediate bond that pulsed between us. Cinco grasped my pinky finger, sending warm energy through my body. His response reassured me that he was with us, and that was all that mattered.

I was lost in the sweet haze of falling in love with my baby when a rumble in my belly signaled impending chaos. A sudden pressure built in my chest, and before I could close my mouth, a loud burp erupted, followed by a torrent of chunky, sour liquid that splattered into my lap. Cliff jumped into action, cupping his hands under my mouth in an attempt to curb the mess as the vomit soaked my gown and lap.

Even though I wasn't ready to leave his side, it was time to lie down. Dizziness began to settle in. My eyes remained fixated on Cinco's body as we left the room.

Many family members made their way to the hospital that day. The gasps of disbelief and barrage of questions that followed the news of the baby's early arrival quickly became overwhelming. "I thought the baby wasn't due for another four months. How did this happen?" they would ask.

We still don't know exactly what caused my body to go into preterm labor. My brief pregnancy had started off normally, with typical lab results coming back clear. I had been getting accustomed to observing my changing body, and excitement was building among family and friends.

This time would be different. I was ready to be a mom. I had chosen a partner who wanted to be a dad and would stick around to care for us all. This was going to be my next best shot at motherhood, even if it meant entering this journey as a young mother.

I knew that one day I would also hold the title of wife. I wanted so badly to be married with kids, to have a good job, and to own a beautiful home. My dreams had evolved, and in my heart, it was finally time to see these dreams come to fruition.

But having a micro-preemie wasn't part of the script I had written.

Cliff and I later pressed the doctors for answers to understand what could have possibly caused his early arrival.

Our inquiries were met with half-hearted responses that only raised more questions. "Maybe you had a virus that triggered your labor. Sometimes things like this can happen even after a full-term pregnancy." Life has a way of surprising you, and Cinco's arrival did just that.

The look on my mom's face as she entered my hospital room reflected fresh shock. I could feel her relief knowing that both of us had made it through labor, but her body also portrayed a story of concern. The wetness from her tears had barely dried by the time she walked in.

I later learned that she had spent time visiting with Cliff and Cinco before coming to see me. This would be the order of events for the day—loved ones would lay their eyes on Cinco and get briefed by Cliff before coming to see me.

Leaving the hospital with an empty womb and car seat shattered my heart. Taking the elevator down to the car alongside a mom who had also been released, cradling her baby in her arms, served as an unwelcome reminder that my dream of a do-over had been crushed. And don't get me started on the uncomfortable interactions I had with people who were aware of my pregnancy but not of Cinco's untimely arrival. I found myself constantly needing to explain why I was no longer pregnant and how he was doing in the NICU.

Before Cinco, I had never been to a NICU or seen so many tiny babies fighting for their lives. I had no idea how many babies were born prematurely to Black women every year or the trials that accompanied having a preemie. Every time the phone rang after ten o'clock, my heart would jump because I feared it would be the call—the call that he had stopped breathing or that something terrible had happened, jeopardizing his chances of coming home. If the unthinkable happened, it would also mean that the fairytale of us being a normal family would never unfold for me.

Cinco was on a ventilator twenty-four seven for the first three months of his life, the machine doing the work for his lungs so they could finish maturing. The natural maturation process had been interrupted by his early arrival.

Holding my baby was always a heavy lift, with multiple nurses preparing us both—maneuvering a million cords and making sure his head was propped up properly on my chest. Each kangaroo swaddle with him laying between my shirt and beating chest was magic for me. It was the next best thing from watching him lay on the bed waiting to be held.

The day finally came for the tubes to be removed, and Cinco transitioned to a nasal cannula, one step closer to eventually getting discharged. JD, Cliff, and I waited at the hospital for several hours that day—waiting for the moment when he could be cradled for the first time. We each took turns holding him, trying our best not to rush each other. This was the first time we could see his now-chubby face without all of the tape. His rosy cheeks matched the warmth in my heart. After some time, we left with plans to return and help with bathtime, a fun pastime for us.

My mom and aunt visited the NICU in between my second visit. She came home with worry in her eyes and said she was terribly concerned with how Cinco was breathing. "Something is wrong babe; he was working too hard to breathe," she shared.

Unable to take any mention of bad news, I brushed her concerns aside and continued with getting dressed to head back out to the hospital. "Mom, everything is fine. They would have called if it wasn't."

Making my way into Cinco's room, my eyes immediately noticed the swarm of doctors surrounding my baby's bed. There were white coats pacing back and forth. His pulmonologist caught sight of my arrival and walked over, catching me midstride to lay eyes on my baby. I needed to see him.

With sadness in his eyes and voice, he said, "I'm so sorry..."

I heard nothing else that came out of his mouth. I shoved him aside and tore my way through the crowd circling Cinco's bed. *Had the unthinkable happened? Was my baby no longer with us?* The thoughts were consuming me one at a time as the fear shut down my senses.

Relief rushed through me as I got a glimpse of Cinco's tiny body fighting as the doctors were trying to intubate him again. His arms were flapping vigorously, his body twisting from side to side. He was still here—thank God—he just needed the tubes back in place for breathing support.

By then the pain and panic of loss had crashed down like a ton of bricks. Any control that I held disappeared, and fury stood in its place. I wanted blood. I called Cliff trying to rope him in on the plan to cause harm to match my pain, to which he declined.

I didn't understand how the doctor could be so careless in his word choice. Everyone knows what it means when a doctor says, "I'm sorry." He tried to explain that he said it that way because he understood how long we had waited for this day to come, and to experience a setback like this was hard.

My relationship with Cliff became strained under the pressures of managing life with a child at home who had needs to be met, while another lived in the NICU. Any time I found a moment to focus on us and nurture what remained of our relationship, I was met with guilt for not being with Cinco.

I got lost in the countless hours of pumping breast milk and being at the hospital, holding my breath as I waited for any moment when it was safe enough to hold him in my arms. Nothing else seemed to matter; I neglected my own health by suspending my maternity leave after five short weeks so that, when he finally came home, I could have the remaining time with him.

Cinco would come off the ventilator for good two days later, after some much-needed steroids. I continued to work my regular shift and headed to the hospital until ten most evenings. This routine came to an end after a grueling 144 days in the NICU, a heart abnormality diagnosis, and two surgeries.

A new routine quickly took its place. My baby came home with a long list of care instructions, countless follow-up visits, twenty-four seven oxygen, and a feeding tube. The round-the-clock care he had received in the hospital was now our full-time responsibility.

He returned to a family that had prayed for his wellbeing but was terribly unprepared for what would be needed to care for him—and for ourselves too.

CHAPTER 11:

Déjà Vu

"Turn it off!" I screamed.

It was 2013, and I was in the truck with JD and Cliff headed to grab dinner. Music was blaring through the truck speakers, and without warning, the lyrics to the song that was playing triggered a memory I'd kept buried deep.

Put Molly all in her champagne, she ain't even know it. I took her home and I enjoyed that, she ain't even know it.

Each line coursed through me as memories from the past flooded my mind. I was twenty-one years old and riding the train to class the day I met him. He worked for the Chicago Transit Authority and struck up a conversation with me as I loaded money onto my transit card. His charm sealed the deal when he asked for my number.

He wasted no time, calling me that same evening, asking if I wanted to hang out and hit up a basketball game, see where the night would lead us. We never made it to dinner and opted to go to a bar instead. The mostly dark, smoky-aired room was filled to the brim with arms swinging and bodies grooving to the music. We ushered our way through the dense crowd to grab a drink. I considered myself an experienced drinker and could easily down two to three vodka cocktails without batting an eye. On a good night, I would accelerate the fun with some tequila shots as chasers.

I'd always hear my mom's words ringing through my ears, "Don't leave your drink unattended, and you and your friends must stay together when out drinking." She was convinced that alcohol had the potential to ruin even a good thing. Me, on the other hand, believed that alcohol doubled the fun, even if it distorted the facts a bit.

"Can I have a vodka with pineapple?" I asked the bartender.

"We don't have pineapple juice. What else do you want?"

I frowned at his flat response. "Got anything citrus?" I replied, irritation simmering under my breath.

A few sips into my drink, the already halfway-lit room began fading into different shades of black. Closing my eyes, white specks of light flashed by like snowflakes. My nerves began to get the best of me. Fearing I might pass out, I excused myself to go to the bathroom.

By the time I made it into the stall, the room was spinning. Thoughts were swirling and slurring in my head. *How could I be so drunk so fast? I hadn't set my drink down—what was happening?*

I stumbled out of the bathroom, needing to hold onto the wall for support.

"Take me home now. I need to go home," I told my date.

The next morning, I peeled open my eyes and scanned the unfamiliar space. A mind-numbing headache pulsated throughout my entire body. I realized I was lying naked in a basement next to the person that I had trusted to take me home.

I slapped his arm to wake him. "I told you to take me home! What happened?" my voice rising frantically.

"Why didn't you take me home?"

His voice was groggy, "What do you mean, what happened? I tried to take you home, but you couldn't walk, so I brought you to my friend's house."

"Did we use a condom?" I asked as I searched the dirty floor for my clothes.

"Uh, yeah," he responded nonchalantly.

"Please just take me home." I had no other words for him during the car ride.

Later, I called my friend Chantel, trying to process what might have happened, but our conversation only resulted in more questions.

"Friend, this doesn't make sense," she said. "Are you sure that you didn't put your drink down?"

I knew I hadn't, but still, the edges of the memory frayed. *Had the bartender messed up my drink? Did I really only have that one drink?*

The word rape never escaped either of our lips. For me, being raped looked like getting snatched from a deserted alley with busted lights hanging from the poles. The person would be a stranger, and violence would most likely ensue, either from him trying to snatch my clothes off or me fighting back.

I decided I needed to call the guy back for answers. I went to meet him at his house with the sole purpose of getting more information. What happened that night was such a blur, and I was consumed with the need for resolution. He was cagey, maintaining that the only thing that happened was that we had sex. Allegedly, I had nearly passed out by the time he got me to the car, which, in his eyes, meant that taking me home wasn't an option.

The visit proved to be futile. I didn't have any more clarity, and I was still unable to wrap my mind around the whole incident. Feelings of embarrassment leaked in. Unable to stomach the confusion and discomfort, I decided to put it down, but only after promising to never talk about it again.

It wasn't until I heard those words assaulting me through the stereo all those years later that I could face what had actually happened to me.

I took her home and I enjoyed that, she ain't even know it. And even though my mind whispered rape, my mouth couldn't yet make the sound. I kept the promise I'd made to myself and still said nothing.

Cliff turned off the song without question. The tension eased in my chest. And we moved forward with our dinner plans.

But I knew I couldn't run forever.

PART 3:

Sinking

CHAPTER 12:

Year of Firsts

I was finally feeling steadier on my feet two years after Cinco's birth when my mom's sickness and then death slapped me squarely in the face. We held her memorial in October 2013, and all of a sudden I had to learn how to be myself again—except I wasn't sure who that person was anymore. How could I move through life without my mom there to help me finish my fights and face my fears? That "year of firsts" was just plain hard. There was no way around it, no matter how much I tried.

God knows I tried.

A few months after her passing, I traveled to New Orleans in an attempt to celebrate my thirtyfourth birthday—my first birthday without her. I inadvertently ended up drinking myself into a stupor, which came with a migraine that wouldn't let up. That morning, I blinked my eyes in disbelief as I stared at the screen on my phone. There, in no uncertain terms, was a text from my mother all the way from heaven.

Happy birthday, dear.

I jumped out of bed with tears in my eyes, not

giving an ounce of thought to how this miracle could have happened. I reread the text over and over again, shouting with joy.

She remembered! I knew it. I am not alone.

My jubilant cries woke my friend, who was not nearly as convinced as I was.

"Friend, I want you to say that again out loud," she prompted me.

"Go on. Say it."

"My mom texted me from heaven," I said firmly.

"Okay, now say it again." She cocked her head to the side, one eyebrow raised.

"My mom texted me from heaven," I insisted.

"Keep saying it."

She made me repeat that same sentence seven times. She said she wanted me to pause and really absorb the words coming out of my mouth, hoping that I would make sense of what had truly happened.

Reality punched me in the gut when the truth set in.

The text had not been sent from heaven. It was from Auntie, who had assumed my mom's number when she died. I had conveniently forgotten about my stubborn decision not to change the name in my phone from Ma to Auntie.

What a cruel and dirty trick, I thought to myself, as the tears soaked my face, and I sat back down on the bed. The delusion was starting to fade, pulling me back down to this hell that I wanted so desperately to escape. I could see how my mind was willing to do anything to make it possible—even bending reality in my favor.

There were other moments of sober remembering.

Like the time I picked up the phone to tell my mom

how a coworker had gotten on my nerves, only to realize that she wouldn't be on the other end to answer. This realization made me angrier than I already was. Why couldn't I hear her voice when I needed it?

I then found myself pissed about Mother's Day coming around the corner, conveniently reminding me that I was a motherless child. Until her death, I had never paid much attention to all of the ads, social media posts, and TV shows celebrating the day. And now, here I was, an outsider.

I spent the greater part of that day rolling around in bed hiding under the covers until my father-in-law called to convince me to join the family for dinner. He, too, unfortunately understood the pain of losing a mom and wanted someone to commiserate with.

When I wasn't spending time being angry, I was pleading with and questioning God. I kept asking Him why He didn't save her. I had asked Him to heal her, not take her. Why did He take her from me? He could've easily taken my dad, who didn't want to be here anyway.

God had instilled my belief in miracles through Cinco's birth journey, but this outcome wasn't what I had in mind for the next miracle. Why had my prayers gone unanswered?

My mom and I had so much life left to live together. We were planning a smash sixtieth birthday party that would never happen. But why? I was desperately seeking answers to explain away my pain. My heart had never felt this type of chronic ache before.

As the first anniversary of her death approached, the world outside my window was turning into a hazy smear of color and sound again. I could feel myself moving clumsily through the days, sticking to the routine as if nothing had changed.

Most mornings, I would wake with heaviness on my chest and tear ducts filled with sadness. On some days, I would surrender to grief, tears spilling down my cheeks. Other days, I concealed the sobs, forcing a smile to take their place. No matter the choice, the relief remained out of reach, like trying to catch clouds with my hands. Deep down, I knew my mom would have encouraged me to keep pushing forward, to find joy, but each step in that direction did nothing to ease the ache of missing her, pulling me further into despair.

I spent the hour-plus commute to and from work straining my voice as I sang through angry tears. Mad at the world, I wasn't equipped to keep living without my mom by my side. When the pain didn't subside and my pleas for answers never came, I kept doing what was in front of me—making it my goal to keep pace with work and ensure that the bills got paid.

I continued this cycle until I heard a voice speak to me while I was asleep sometime in late July 2014. You know the tone a mom uses when she tells her kid to jump down from the slide at the playground, holding space for their fear while believing they can achieve the unthinkable? It felt like that. While the voice that spoke to me felt masculine, there was that same sense of promise as the mother's voice.

"You already know what you need to do," it said firmly.

I sprang from the mattress as if a cord had pulled me upward. With my eyes open, I uttered the words aloud, "Are you sure?"

I immediately knew the message was connected to the dissatisfaction I'd been experiencing at work. I was now managing a large community clinic, and the impact of bringing healthcare services to communities that needed them most no longer stirred the fire in my heart like it once did. Unbeknownst to others, the long drives, days jammed with meetings, and constant problem solving had worn me down. The fulfillment I once felt had left me entirely.

Also, somewhere deep, missing my mom so much increased my hunger to be more present with my boys. In order for that to happen, something needed to give. Quitting my job felt like low-hanging fruit to cut out of my life. The knots in my belly began to multiply rapidly, and dubious thoughts started to seep in.

How will this work? What will people think? I closed my eyes again, stillness draping over me. The voice was right; I knew that the time had come to quit.

There was nothing I could do to calm the uncertainty that would come with this decision, but the time to act was now. Intuitively, I knew what I had been doing wasn't bringing happiness my way. Making this decision meant trying something different, possibly giving myself the freedom to detach from any notions tied to a specific outcome. I would leap off the cliff and deal with whatever was coming, whenever it came.

At that time, I didn't know what I had done to bring the voice to me. Struck by its clarity, I made the decision to submit my resignation letter by the end of the week. There would be no bargaining or shopping this idea around to others before deciding.

A few days later, I walked into my boss's office with my resignation letter in hand. "What's this?" she asked, mouth agape.

Up until this point in our relationship, I had struck her as a pretty logical person. I had been working there for almost six years and had been promoted twice—coming in as a coordinator and climbing my way up to an operations director.

"So, what will you do? Do you have a job lined up?" she asked, looking for answers.

This quitting business didn't make sense to her, nor to my family and friends with whom I had already shared my plans. What she didn't know was that I had been job seeking and interviewing for several months. Although the voice had prompted me to take the leap and actually leave this job, the idea wasn't new to me. I'd been trying to line up something else for a while.

Sometimes I'd make it to the last round before hearing the words, "We are going to go with another candidate." A brief sulking period would ensue before I could pull myself together again to take a swing at the next opportunity. My job had to be out there; I just had to keep fighting until I couldn't anymore.

"I'm going to spend some time figuring out what I need to do next. I just need to leave, and that's all I know." It was a canned response I had been using to address the barrage of questions that came my way whenever I shared the news of my sudden departure with any of my family or friends.

Looking back, they were right to be incredulous. I had always tried my best to color within the lines when it came to my professional self. I followed the rules and modeled the behavior I wanted my team to exhibit. I was predictable;

this was part of my conditioning and the values instilled in me. My mom would work a job until she couldn't anymore, showing up early and leaving after quitting time.

"You don't leave a job until you have another lined up.

This is the way you do it," she would tell me.

Interestingly, Cliff was the only person who was both surprised and supportive of my choice as the words came out of my mouth. Unlike everyone else, he'd had a front-row seat to the deconstructing process that had been taking place and was the only person who knew how much I needed something to change. I didn't realize at the time that the hole in my heart was growing in proportion to my inability to keep things the same.

The news of my impending departure spread through the organization like wildfire. I informed my team with tears streaming down my face during an impromptu staff meeting. We had become a family over the years, learning how to work together to serve a community that we all cared about.

In an effort not to leave the team in the lurch, I extended my departure date to three weeks out. To my surprise, this time passed quickly, and with it, the pressure that I had once felt in my chest began to wane. My charge was clear—I was there to wrap things up. My job of building and fixing had been completed. I made it a point to end my days on time and prioritize attending JD's baseball games during the week.

I even started daydreaming about how I would spend my time between jobs. Perhaps I would nap during the day and take Cinco to the park to play while I looked for jobs that were closer to home. The excitement of the unknown intrigued me; I never once experienced the worry that had become second nature. For the first time in my life, I wasn't anxious about how I would pay the bills or when my next dollar would come. I was able to allow myself to be present and accept that I was exactly where I needed to be.

While working from home one day, I received an email from someone named Jayson Bird. I had heard the name and knew that we worked for the same organization, but at another location. We had never met or even exchanged an email until now. His message was short and vague, asking if I was interested in a leadership role at the local health department and to send my resume.

My heart pounded as I reread the covert message over and over again. How could they be hiring? I had applied several times for jobs and endured what were horrible interview experiences before being told, "Nah." I quickly checked the department website and couldn't find the open role. Out of pure curiosity, I emailed him back, expressing my interest along with my resume, and proceeded to move on with my day.

Thirty short minutes later, I answered a call from the health department's first deputy, asking me to come in for an interview with him and the medical director. A wave of shock came over after I hung up the phone. The timing was impeccable; I was able to walk away from my current job with a scheduled interview.

There was no way that this was happening. A job interview just landed in my lap. I had been working feverishly to secure interviews, and this one felt like it had fallen from the sky.

I cried like a baby on my last day of work. There was no turning back from my decision to leave. These weren't tears of sadness, but of relief. All I had to do was stay focused on how I would fill my days during this break and prepare myself to knock this interview out of the park.

As I slipped into my tailored black suit, I could feel my confidence moving up my backbone. The crisp white shirt was a striking contrast for my brown skin. My outfit was complete with black high heels that made an impression whenever I walked into a room. Looking like a million bucks, I'd been briefed on important details like the date, the interview time, the place, and who I was meeting with. There was only one missing piece—I didn't know anything about the job.

It was another first for me. Without the specifics, there was no real way for me to prepare. My usual routine was anticipating every question they would ask and writing down meticulous notes of the many ways I could respond. I'd spend tons of time dissecting the company website, doing mock interviews with friends, and practicing facial expressions in the mirror.

I had no intel that I could leverage in the pursuit of increasing my blood pressure and coming off as a nervous wreck to a future employer. What I had in my hands this round, beneath the nerves, were experiences and stories about my accomplishments waiting to be shared.

Wasting no time, the first deputy jumped in asking, "What do you know about the role?" His question hung in the air, as I prepared to share my truth.

"All I know is that this is an administrative role, and I am truly honored to have the opportunity to be interviewed today."

Seemingly unbothered by my response, he moved on. "This role will be in the executive office, overseeing a team of thirty to forty people providing mental health services."

Yes, mental health was my jam. I chimed in to

share my experiences in overseeing clinical operations for the past six years, where mental health was a part of the offerings. As each question came my way, my thoughts quickly crystallized in my mind and came out racing to be heard. I shocked myself as the clarity in my voice began to grow steadier with each sentence. The self-doubt that I once felt coming into this room had dissipated.

I was embracing a version of myself that I never knew existed, which also meant that there were multiple instances when I had to anchor my feet to the floor and fight the urge to float away, as my mind tried its best to keep pace with details as they emerged. Somewhere in between the end of the interview and the request for me to meet with the commissioner that same day, I was informed that, if hired, the role came with a six-figure salary—doubling what I had earned in my previous role.

The butterflies in my belly were salsa dancing as I left the health department. Hearing the commissioner say, "I am looking forward to working with you. You will hear something on Friday," was enough for me to know that I had this one in the bag.

CHAPTER 13:

New Dawn

I was free! I could hardly believe that I was unemployed and able to direct how I would spend my time. The government hiring process would take some time, and I reassured myself that this would only be for a couple of months. There was no way I could be off longer than that. I mean, how would we survive if I didn't start my new job by the end of the year? This was the right move for now. However, self-talk alone wasn't enough to ease the negative thoughts creeping in and out of my subconscious.

I mostly spent my newfound freedom in bed; I was exhausted. Since it was summer, we didn't have to deal with the demands of school drop-offs. I slept in until after ten each morning and went to bed whenever my eyes felt like closing for the day. Cliff was a champ, holding down the fort with the boys while I focused on giving my body the space to recover. Even after all that sleep, the achiness and grogginess that accompanies exhaustion remained.

When I wasn't sleeping, I enjoyed picnics and playdates at the park with the boys. I played photographer as they rode their bikes. Seeing the joy on their faces and hearing their laughter made this time together so precious.

In those moments, I was reminded of what I had been missing out on—face-to-face time with my boys that I would never be able to get back. This was my opportunity to make up for lost time and think about how my next move would need to align with having a more physical presence with them. I wanted more money, time with family and friends, and meaningful impact in my next role.

I reconnected with friends through long phone calls about anything and everything, chatty dinners, and boozy brunches. I shared details about what I had been up to, how I had heard the voice, and the reasons behind my departure. In return, I was able to catch up and have more capacity to be present for moments like birthdays, fielding calls about a crazy-ass boyfriend or coworker, or just going out for desserts and enjoying a few words in between bites. This time felt like it was mine to direct and own.

I was met with love and support, which felt like confirmation that I was on the right path. For as long as I could remember, I'd always been consumed with how others saw me and whether what I was doing was right. Both deeply mattered to me, and I had become woefully aware of how I had allowed the voices of others to infiltrate my thoughts and guide my behaviors. This time, I moved on the voice's promise and tried to push my old ways of being aside.

I found Cliff to be both kind and patient with me. It was as if he placed our collective troubles on the shelf and focused his energy on making sure I felt cared for.

I remembered this Cliff—the man I first met and the same one who swaddled me with his love after

Cinco had been born. During my time off, he ran my bathwater and continued to pour loving words into my soul. He helped the stress melt down my shoulders, allowing them to rest away from their usual position clenched and tucked under my ears.

"I love you, babe. You made the right decision. It's so good to have you home more," he would say often. His words calmed my thoughts of uncertainty about the future, helping to create a wedge between the internal tensions of knowing I was where I needed to be and the ticking clock urging a swift resolution from the human resource's long vetting process.

In my heart, I knew the job was mine, and yet I still managed to be unsure of myself. It wouldn't be real until I got the official word. Yes, all of the signs were pointing in my favor, but given the ease of this process (beyond the painful waiting), I was still holding my breath, waiting for the bottom to fall out.

About a month into my break, the official word came through, but it would be at least another month before I could start, allowing me additional time to tackle another critical tension building in the background. The one-year anniversary of my mom's death was making its way to the calendar. I wanted to celebrate her existence and the miracle of me still clawing my way through life. Talking to a couple of friends encouraged me to bring my loose celebration idea to life by booking a five-night girls' trip to Miami.

Luckily, I wasn't the only one lurking around for some fun and release. This trip would also serve as a birthday celebration for the friend whose birthday dinner I was attending when I received the news about the oxygen troubles that ultimately preceded my mom's last short days in hospice.

This getaway came at the right time. The warmth of the Miami sun hitting my skin felt like a soothing balm. We laid on the beach for countless hours, danced our butts off in the clubs, laughed until our bellies ached, and cried together about the events of yesterday. Rounds of flowing drinks helped to bring light to my regrets about not getting a second opinion after my mom's cancer diagnosis. Internally, I had been fighting with not making decisions that could have made all of the difference and kept my mom here with me, causing all of the questioning and "what ifs" to come into view.

Why hadn't I been smart enough to consider our options or take her someplace that was world-renowned for the type of cancer she had? I just went with whatever had been presented to us without thinking about her quality of life, which I had known since I was a child was important to her. How did I miss this crucial piece? Was my lapse in judgment the missing factor that could have changed the outcome and transformed the puzzle image into something sweeter? Would my mom still be here with me?

My friends did their best to calm my circular, damning, and sometimes-drunken thought patterns. Unable to provide answers that pacified me, they helped me see the benefit of shifting my focus to the here and now. Facing the hard truth that this reality was mine to work through and that looking backward with blame leading the charge would only bring more suffering.

The late beach nights listening to and watching the waves move into an unforeseeable distance helped transport me above the pain, if only for a moment. This imagery signified that there was more out there for me, even if I couldn't see it now.

An evening reflection session on the beach resulted in making plans for the future—like deciding to pursue a doctorate in the coming year, making a personal commitment to always celebrate my mom's life every year, and working on accepting my mom's departure as final. There would be no more going back in time trying to rewind the hands. All I had was today.

I returned home from my vacation with fire in my bones and a renewed capacity to tackle my new gig. I had survived the hardest days of that year and held tightly onto the hope that everything would be more than okay.

CHAPTER 14:

One Plus One Equals Three

Cliff and I were alone watching the midday news when he turned toward me and casually asked, "Do you still want to get married?"

I jumped from the bed to get a clear view of his face and body language. I needed to read every nuance of his expression.

"Are you for real? You want to get married?" I could hardly believe what I was hearing.

Smiling at my excitement, Cliff nodded yes.

There was no ring, no getting down on one knee, but I didn't care. I had no other questions. Him approaching me to get married after so many arguments and years of waiting was more than enough to start planning. All I knew was that my time to shine had arrived.

Days into our engagement, I was springing into action mode—trying to nail down dates and thinking through all the other parties and celebrations that automatically came with getting married. Three months slipped through my fingers, and gratefully, I experienced a fun-filled bachelorette party with the girls before my doctor's words cut through any excitement I had left.

"The test is positive."

I had come in to see her because of relentless migraines that commanded dark rooms and motionless naps. This visit was supposed to lay out the many medication options before getting my script and walking out the door. Oh, and I was also going to get a new prescription for birth control pills. That task had been on my to-do list for a while but had fallen by the wayside.

Reminiscent of a seventeen-year-old me, I asked, "Can I take another test? There was another lady in the lab—maybe there was a mixup."

"Yeah, she's pregnant too," my doctor said with a chuckle. Sensing the sincerity in my request and growing impatient with my denial, she instructed, "This will be the last test. And I will perform it myself."

I was convinced that something was amiss. Yes, Cliff and I were having sex sparingly, but not nearly enough to make a whole baby. And with these thirty-five-year-old ovaries, there was no way.

"See, it's positive again," she said, showing me the test in her hand. My knees started shaking as I sat on the table, dread seeping into my being.

I had just started my new job at the health department less than six months ago. The digital ink on my recently submitted doctoral school application had barely dried.

My belly was still brewing with hunger to learn more after completing my master's degree, and with this hunger came an impenetrable belief that gaining a doctorate would help to open new doors and take my career to new heights.

I had different plans for what the rest of this year would look like. I was hellbent on being present at work, starting school, and becoming mom of the year. Work was kicking my ass; this was my first go in government, and the culture was getting the best of my strategic skills. I needed more time and focus to wrap my head around this big job.

As for school, if it happened, I convinced myself that I would be ready to take the opportunity with open arms.

Plus, I had grown accustomed to carrying heavy loads to achieve my dreams. Doing all of this while pregnant or with a newborn attached to my nipples was not on the vision board.

"When was your last period?" my doctor piped in, jolting me back into reality and out of my swirling thoughts.

Tracking periods were a thing of the past. For the last several years, my cycles came when they wanted, with or without birth control. There was no way I could come up with a date for her.

A physical exam revealed that I could be at least eight or nine weeks pregnant. My doc moved on to suggesting that I see someone who specializes in high-risk pregnancies. She had been along for the ride with Cinco and wanted me to be proactive in preventing lightning from striking twice.

Eagerly waiting for her to leave, I called Cliff as I got dressed. The line had barely clicked when I blurted out, "I'm pregnant"—the words hanging like dirty laundry on the line for everyone to see.

I could both feel and hear his smile through the phone. "We will always be poor. I didn't commit to a life of poverty," I continued, my voice unable to mask the tightness building in my chest.

His voice remained calm as he asked that we meet

for breakfast before I headed into the office. Glancing at the clock and recognizing how I'd lost track of time, what was one more hour in the grand scheme? We agreed to meet at a restaurant that would place me closer to work.

Before disconnecting the call, Cliff made another attempt to ease my fears. "Everything is going to be okay, babe."

He was way too calm for my taste, so I called another friend on my way to the car. The frigid wind stung my once-warm cheeks, freezing the tears before they could fall. The negative twenty-eight-degree wind chill wasn't a factor as I unleashed my fears into the phone.

"We are going to be poor forever! This can't be the plan that God had in mind for me. Having Cinco nearly killed me and Cliff. How could I ever make this work? And what if I get into the doctoral program? School starts in August, and if my doctor is correct, this baby is coming this year!" My friend, a gentle soul, did her best to listen and not laugh at what must have sounded like pure hysteria. I could feel the desperation chasing me down as I searched my purse for my now-lost parking ticket. This shit storm was blurring my thoughts and made simple tasks into a mountain. I stood next to my car and listened as my friend guided my steps on what to do next.

"First things first, you won't live in poverty. It's not your fate. Get your behind in the car before you freeze to death. Everything is going to work out. Drive up to the gate and talk to the attendant. They will understand about losing your ticket. I can stay on the phone with you. Go and talk to Cliff and figure out the plan. Friend, everything will work out. It always does."

I am forever grateful for making that call. Her

ability to stop whatever she was doing to drop a lifeline my way was exactly what I needed to get out of that lot and reconcile the contradicting thoughts for the conversation ahead.

Bringing another child into this world felt like stepping on a tightrope without a safety net. The absence of my mother pulled on my heartstrings. Becoming a mom again without her was never the plan for me.

However, the thought of having another abortion felt like a distant afterthought, drowned out by the promise I made to embrace motherhood again while trying to conceive Cinco. We fought so hard to keep him here; making that choice again could come with consequences that my heart couldn't hold.

Cliff did most of the talking at breakfast. His comforting words did little to ease the tangled knots in my belly. Our reactions to the news highlighted the distance between our respective outlooks. His excitement overshadowed the guilt gnawing at my organs as I sobbed thinking about the neglected plans and months that I'd let slip by without making that birth control appointment until it was too late.

Sharing happy news while feeling sad felt foreign, so I held the news of my pregnancy close until after my first OB appointment. The cool gel sent chills as the ultrasound screen showed arms waving like tiny branches. Selfishly, I was hoping to see a tadpole, not a full-blown baby. Having another child still felt so nebulous, and I envisioned the tech needing to describe the contents of an abstract image. Instead, I could clearly see my baby baking in my womb.

Somehow, I was a full twelve weeks pregnant.

I'd snoozed through the whole first trimester. How

in the hell did I become one of those women that I used to suspect was lying about not knowing about being pregnant until the baby slid out one day?

With just a handful of months before our baby made his debut, Cliff and I got married at the courthouse on a rainy Friday morning. Cliff would tell the world that we were one, and I would finally have my dreams of being a wife fulfilled.

I wore a flowy white gown that swayed, a perfect fit for my rounded belly, cradling son number three. With warm, springlike hues brushed across my cheeks, my face caught the light, enhancing my pregnancy glow. Bright red lipstick traced across my lips, making a bold statement against my soft gown. My mother's black crochet shawl draped around my shoulders to remind me of her embrace.

Cliff was dressed sharp as a tack wearing a charcoal suit, a white button-up, and a navy tie with white polka dots. A fresh lining complemented his wavy Caesar cut.

The courtroom was filled with laughter and tears, as family and friends encircled and the judge read the vows. I could hear the camera shutter clicks and sniffles in between his words. We stood shoulder to shoulder, as Cliff gently held and stroked my hands so that I could feel his heart. For a brief moment, looking into his eyes, it was just the two of us soaking up the charge of becoming one.

The anticipation for a brighter future together was Mount Everest high. My acceptance letter into the program came days later and was a highlight of a challenging pregnancy. I spent more than half of it working from home due to my body showing signs of an early delivery.

As weeks turned into months, the walls of our duplex became a sanctuary against the pressure of having another preemie. After the fraught experience with Cinco, every additional day with my baby in the womb felt like a victory. When the doctor agreed to lift some restrictions, I rejoiced in knowing that we were just a bit closer to having him make a safe entrance.

With determination leading the way, I approached HR with a request to take an extended maternity leave. The prospect of those days being filled with coos and sleepy snuggles was too good to pass up. He would be our last little one, and four months away from work would give us bonding time that I could never get back.

Emory came into the world lungs ablaze; his unrelenting cries pierced the room. I can still see Cliff glowing with anticipation as our little one made his debut. We were surrounded by love with JD and Auntie also sharing in the miracle of childbirth. JD spontaneously became a videographer and photographer, helping to create a time capsule that we could revisit and one day share with Emory.

Hot tears poured down my cheeks, a release that can only come after a week-long hospital stay, attending my first day of class, and twelve hours of grueling labor. My body felt like an accomplished, fragile vessel—strained and relieved.

Emory's tiny body, still sticky from birth, squirmed as I held him tightly for the first time. As I cradled him, our cries ceased, and a primal connection settled in. I could feel his heart beating against mine as I watched Cliff's steady hands cut the umbilical cord and a smile come over his face—similar to the one he flashed at breakfast just six months earlier.

CHAPTER 15:

She's the Boss

Being a mom of three wore me down in every way.

Exhaustion had turned into the Grim Reaper, hell-bent on trying to break me. The long nights of reading and writing papers for school, along with full days of breastfeeding and the struggles of showing up for my other two children, fractured my back in at least six places.

Three months into my maternity leave, I was growing itchy and ready for a change of pace. Thankfully, the universe responded with an earlier-than-expected start date for Emory's daycare. I happily jumped on the opportunity.

The never-ending cycles of change over the past several months had knocked me sideways, and I was desperately seeking something that could steady me. While work came with its challenges, it also served as an anchor of routine that I came to rely on.

In addition to welcoming a new family member, our living situation had changed as well. During my pregnancy, we had moved into a new place far on the other side of town. We were in search of more space and better schools, and we were eager for a slower-paced environment to raise the boys. This new home had moved us even further from family and friends and resulted in a longer commute for Cliff and me. We quickly became passing ships in the night, making sporadic, tactical calls to each other during the day to keep our many household duties afloat.

"Hey, have you thought about dinner tonight?" "Can you pick up both boys today?"

Handling what was in front of us became routine, our means to just get through. Cinco's health had become harder to manage. Asthma attacks were picking up, increasing our reliance on emergency room visits, hospital stays, and specialty care. His already long list of follow-up visits over the years had now expanded to include routinely seeing a cardiologist and pulmonologist to monitor the confluences of his heart abnormality and asthma and determine the optimal time for heart surgery to take place. This cruel waiting game played tricks on my mind.

There were times when I was excited to hear that we had another year, leading me to think maybe surgery would never be needed. Perhaps Cinco was a rare bird whose very existence defied all logic. Unfortunately, these feelings of relief were fleeting and rudely interrupted when the next visit rolled around and the doctor conveniently reminded me of the real plan.

The load that Cliff and I were carrying was getting heavier. Even though we both acknowledged that all this adult business was getting in the way of anything spontaneous or fun in our lives, I took no action to change it. I had other fish to fry.

Two years into my government gig, I was ready to jump into something new and started putting myself out there again. Similar to previous experiences, I'd find myself making it to the last stages of interviews before losing out to another candidate. The flow of denials coming my way fueled my desire to leave this job even more. An exit sign flashed in my brain weekly, sometimes daily. This annoyance morphed into an obsession that infiltrated my thoughts and created an undeniable urgency.

No one mentioned to me that my portfolio responsibilities would grow to first match and then exceed my newly doubled income. I struggled to balance pressures from the mayor's office, personnel issues, and the timely completion of tasks. Contending with migraine headaches and eating tears for lunch with my office door closed became a new norm.

The budget discussions at work bled into the taxing conversations I was having at home with Cliff. The narrative wasn't too dissimilar. There was more work to do than we could comfortably afford, bringing about more stress. My personal debt was growing by the second and influenced my spending decisions in ways that made sense and others that did not.

Sometimes I could go months without splurging on something I wanted. And then, boom, a bad workday or week could result in multiple, consecutive, out-of-control shopping sprees. I bought whatever tickled my fancy—a $500 bag or $200 jeans often did the trick.

At other times, I became a socialite, flashing my new goods. I had an insatiable desire to be out in the streets, hanging with friends, and experiencing lavish dinners filled with as many appetizers and cocktails as my raging credit card balance could handle. Getting at least a little tipsy was always the goal, and I couldn't go home until that job was done.

I routinely and publicly blamed Cliff for our money

woes. He was the one who agreed to buy the fancy appliances or purchase new wardrobes for the kids at Christmas time. I convinced myself that the money challenges were at the root of our marital mishaps. Our life was far outpacing the bank account and cramping my style. The only answer to this jam was to make more money.

Sometimes drunken, negative thoughts about my marriage seeped into my psyche without permission, helping to suppress my faith that I could see this relationship through. My concerns grew enough for me to question if I had the ability to push myself up the "hillside of happiness," or if that hillside was even within the realm of physical possibilities. My boys deserved to see their mom happy, and I desperately wanted them to experience happiness during their childhood. Cinco was now eight, Emory four.

JD, well into his life journey, had left for college in New Jersey two years prior to pursue his dreams of becoming a successful lawyer. His departure unexpectedly yanked my heartstrings in several directions. I was both ecstatic for him and also worried about his safety and how the world would treat him in my absence.

Could my dream of wanting the world to be kinder to him than he could ever be to it become a reality? Would he know what to do if he ever got into a jam with the police? Could he manage cleaning his dorm and tackling piles of dirty laundry? Who would be there to remind him to eat in the morning and again at dinner?

JD's physical absence intensified my wish to make the best of the shoddy relationship that I held with my dad.

Brief, funny phone calls on our respective birthdays and holidays served as the thread holding our connection intact.

"Hey Dad, just calling to say happy birthday and I love you! Do you have any plans to celebrate?"

In response, he'd say, "Punkin, yeah, it's a national holiday. It's good to hear from you. I wish you would call me more."

I was grateful that he always sounded happy to talk to me, no matter who initiated the call. Unfortunately, these calls also became a source of sadness for me. They often ended with him making what I call "half-hearted" plans to see me and the boys. He would restate his interest in getting to know them and in carving out special time for just us two, but never quite deliver.

His vision saw us having a night out on the town. The highlight would be a fancy dinner, where he would foot the bill, and I could have whatever I wanted. "Punkin, you get ready for that dinner, daughter. It's coming soon," he'd promise before ending the call. By now, the adult version of me had come to see that my dad was only good with one part of promises—making them.

Life wasn't only happening to me; peers around me were losing loved ones. My already fractured back—the result of my own misery—also allowed life challenges experienced by others to widen the window into my own pain.

A former high school classmate buried his sixteen-year-old son after a fatal asthma attack. That news felt like a hard hammer breaking both my knees, causing me to spiral into all the "what ifs." Cinco also has asthma—could God be that cruel and take him from me after all we've been through? What would I do?

Around the same time, a coworker shared that his mother had died before he could make it back to Haiti to see her. He had been making plans for months and continually put them off. The hollowness in his voice over the phone was enough to rumble my insides and awaken dull pain from my mother's death.

I had been trying to figure out how to take small steps toward healing the pain in my heart stemming from her sudden absence, which had taken my breath away. Images of her face crossed my mind most days, and memories of fun times began to make me giggle a little. My heart didn't ache as much, but its existence still lingered within me.

When the fifth Mother's Day without my mom on Earth rolled around, I noticed that it was better than the first, and perhaps the previous year, as well. It felt good to have JD home and to celebrate with all three boys. Cliff, however, was tuned into another radio station that day—treating it just like any other day. There were no mushy or sweet elements to brighten the day or my spirit. The fiery anger already growing in my belly grew at least two feet in those twenty-four hours.

The practice of journaling felt like a natural landing space for me to document the various tensions tugging at me, clouding my judgment, and forcing my hand to behave like a tyrant. I experienced some relief by expelling some of the madness stewing inside me. I desperately craved the lightness in my shoulders after each session, even if only for a brief moment.

There was nothing like coming home after a long day at work and curling up on the bed to pop open my journal and write whatever spilled out of my brain without restraint. By this time, my journal entries had become more candid and lacked the discretion I had previously used to color situations for the sake of maintaining some privacy. While some secrets needed to remain just that, I wasn't holding back from myself anymore.

This internal work helped me to see how I had become a witness to all the drama playing out like a Lifetime movie. I had been removing myself from the writer's room and operating more like a producer—ensuring that the actors continued to align their actions with the script that I had so artfully created. Even in the producer's seat, I recognized that the script had been riddled with desires that had been informed by rage-filled shouting matches with Cliff and what society told me I needed.

Despite this truth, there were glimpses of goodness hiding in plain sight, neatly placed in between the madness. I held the responsibility of zooming out and shifting my perspective to see things in another light. On February 12, 2018, I wrote:

I'm 38 now! Just had to say that—put it in writing again. It's time for new approaches to age-old and new problems. Today was an interesting one. It's a city-reserved holiday, which means I was off but very much on. There's so much to do, but goodness is tucked in there somewhere. I'm on a good path—I just need to pivot to tell the 'right' story. I'm honestly feeling overwhelmed with everything on my plate. Work is hectic, but for all the same and wrong reasons. There's no changing the same old thing, but changing my frame and attitude is key. As much as I want out, something is fostering in my ambivalence

*that I can't shake or put my finger on. I'm ready for
something new—I want*

*to position myself for something grand and be excited
about my next move. I've done the 'not-so-excited-
about-that-gig' thing before. Need I remind myself
how that went? I was miserable there! But that was
a different time and a different me, personally and
professionally.*

These entries also served as powerful declarations
of promises I made to myself to be better and reminders
that there was always a tomorrow to look forward to,
even in the face of gloomy days. All I had to do was
keep an open mind, ground myself in what I know,
and articulate my needs in a meaningful way. Oh, I
needed to learn how to forgive and move on, working
through the tears and fear that were starting to cripple
me. Although my situation was painful and disap-
pointing now, I could move on. Brighter days had to
be on the horizon for this girl.

After an almost two-year job search, I eventually
clawed my way out of a government job and into
a high-powered role in an organization focused on
women's issues. I became their first Black woman
leader. The time had come for me to shrink my portfolio
and lean into the issue areas that were important to me.
I was excited about the potential for enacting change
and bringing forth the impact that I had struggled so
hard to achieve in my current role.

My departure from the city gig was surprisingly
bittersweet as I started to wind down my duties
and reflect on what I had accomplished. I felt loved
through the warm wishes of colleagues expressing
sadness about my impending absence. I had indeed

made a difference and touched others despite my own beliefs. My time there was meaningful. It afforded me the opportunity to stretch professionally and meet amazing people, many of whom I still hold friendships with to this day.

When the day came for me to start my new job, I was so excited that I couldn't sleep. I began that first day with an energy deficit due to the eagerness that had kept me up that night. My mind just couldn't settle down. I was ready to dive in. The anticipation of setting new plans and executing them was intoxicating.

This role would be a coming out party for me. I had never led an organization before and felt an intense responsibility of leading with integrity and intentionality. It was my time to take everything I'd learned throughout my career and stand in the sun.

The early days were fast-paced and jam-packed with meetings, getting to know what felt like thousands of people and peeling back the curtains to reveal the many unknown challenges that awaited my arrival. There were fires big and small that required my attention, causing these days to sometimes span ten to twelve hours. A lot of that time was spent thinking, assessing, and strategizing pathways forward.

I quickly learned that some team members and several board members were happier about my arrival than others, making the office door a revolving one. I wasn't used to people being unenthusiastic when they saw me coming or hearing about their disbelief in my leadership capabilities directly from their mouths to my ears.

Although I had strong support from loved ones, I couldn't help but let these situations spur thoughts of incompetence and uneasiness about my decision to take on this challenge. What was I thinking in taking on a role this large, especially given all the things already stacked on my plate? What did I really know about fundraising? Had I jumped from the frying pan into the fire?

The uneasiness felt at work and ongoing pressures to release some of the tension at home helped to solidify the decision to take on couples counseling. I was already up to my neck, feeling like I could explode at any second—something had to give.

CHAPTER 16:

Exposed

The decision to partake in couples counseling happened sometime in mid 2018. Cliff and I were at odds about everything—from my pining for him to become an active participant in our marriage to his wish for me to stop picking fights with him. We were bleeding all over each other and bringing more harm than we could handle into the relationship.

Finding our therapist involved little-to-no research by two nearly despondent individuals. A simple Google search and a list of therapists in our insurance network were just enough to get us in front of someone—someone, albeit experienced, who looked like us.

Personally, I was seeking relatability and a person outside of our relationship to finally tell Cliff to get his act together. I was tired of handling this matter alone; I needed some reinforcement. Maybe hearing the same thing from a paid professional would reach him in ways that I couldn't.

I was excited about our first visit. Finally, I could get some things off my chest with someone who could actually help me do it. We rode the train downtown together and talked very little during the nearly sixty-minute ride. My excitement was heightened by the potential that this session could bring.

Immediately after arriving at the office, my smile faded when I saw what looked like an angry couple waiting to go back. I leaned into Cliff, somewhat happy that we were still capable of hiding our negative emotions in public. Things hadn't gotten that bad; pretending in front of others was common for us.

Neil, the only brown therapist available from the small pool at this practice, emerged from a side door that led to his office. It was a quaint space with minimal room between the desk chair and the loveseat. The furniture was nestled on a multicolored rug, and there were a couple of bookcases filled with various titles. A window on the left wall provided a glimpse of the blue skies awaiting us after the session.

Maybe we should make plans to grab dinner and discuss the session, I thought to myself.

Neil was not what I expected. He lacked presence and slouched his broad shoulders as he walked. He was over six feet tall and wore loosely-fitted work clothes that concealed his thin frame. His half-wrinkled, nude-colored, button-up shirt was tucked into dark gray slacks that draped down to his brown shoes, held up by a brown belt. His eyes met the clock hanging above us as he looked upward before starting to speak. "So, tell me your names and how you both met," he began.

Neil had no idea the muddy waters he stepped into with this question. To his detriment, he gestured for Cliff to go first.

Cliff 's story always loosely mirrored mine regarding the details of where we went, who was there, and the phone call afterward. When he started to describe his lack of interest in me and how I was all over him is when things usually began to go south. I would always start off laughing when Cliff would tell his version; then the fury would begin to heat up my nerves—the bad ones.

Let's be clear—I was way too cool to be all over Cliff that first night. Was I expressing interest by smiling and asking questions? Yes, I was.

Feeling the smoke creeping up my neck, I passed on the opportunity to tell my side of the story. Neil decided we should move on to why we were there.

Now we are getting down to business, I thought.

I was eager to jump in and share how Cliff had checked out of our marriage, leaving me to shoulder an unreasonable share of the load. His financial situation had sporadic wins—moments when he could contribute to paying our growing monthly expenses. Then, without warning or follow up, the money would be gone and the commitments to do better next time would show up. This back and forth increased my self-reliance and lessened my belief in Cliff 's ability to take care of us if I ever fell down completely. The feelings of not needing him heightened, while pieces of me still wanted him to swoop in and save the day.

"We had made tons of plans, only to have them all fall through because of him," were the first of many words that tumbled out of my mouth. "I don't trust him at all because he's let me down too many times. I have a terrible relationship with my dad, who also lets me down often. He's an addict and hasn't been able to show me the love I've always wanted and needed. I'm pissed at them all."

I didn't stop there; I couldn't help myself.

"My romantic relationships have done nothing but

hurt me. Cliff is no different from the others; I thought I got it right this time. However, all I do is yell, and all we do is argue. I'm tired and need help. I'm here because we need assistance to fix this; we aren't able to talk calmly to each other about difficult things."

Neil tried to politely cut me off without success. It wasn't until I took a breath from airing my grievances that he was able to pose the same question to Cliff, whose response was straightforward. "I'm here because she told me I had to come." His posture had grown limp, and what looked like disinterest was pasted all over his face.

I knew this version of Cliff well too—when his hearing became selective and he scoped the joint for an exit. I loathed this Cliff because he lacked any fight that matched mine, and it bred fear that he would check out of the marriage before me. There was no way he could peace out before I was ready for him to.

Smoke from my heated body struck fire and started to fill the room. My eyes had turned into lasers that tried to burn holes into Cliff's body whenever I looked in his direction. I wanted to make sure he knew how mad I was. He deserved to feel my wrath. And yet, he skillfully kept his cool, making it nearly impossible for me to gauge how he was feeling, which pissed me off even more. If only I had more intel, I could do more harm in that moment.

Neil fidgeted in his seat, glancing nervously at the clock, his pen pausing mid-sentence. I could almost hear the gears turning in his brain as he struggled to take stock of our issues. As soon as the clock struck the fifty-minute mark, Neil stopped the session and asked when we could come back again. According to him, that session was when we could dig deeper into why we were in therapy.

I couldn't get out of that office fast enough. I needed to be away from them both. Neil was an asshole for treating my marriage like a damn basketball game. Cliff was an asshole for not taking therapy seriously. *Really, Cliff? You are only here because I told you to be?* My mind was spinning in several directions at once. *So, you don't need to be here for our family to fix all the shit you broke?*

The hallway elevator morphed into a boxing ring, with us as opponents in our separate corners. I paused my stride as the doors opened to allow Cliff to go ahead of me. Once we hit the frigid outdoors, I made it a point to go in the opposite direction from Cliff. I walked in the cold, tears pouring down my face, and the crisp wind stabbing at me, chills rolling down my body.

Meeting a girlfriend for happy hour would be how I ended the day after completing my very first ever therapy session. I sent an unanswered text to Cliff to inform him that I would be late and that he would be responsible for the boys tonight. The drinks and tears flowed as I recounted the details.

I wish I could say that subsequent sessions with Neil ended more pleasantly than the first. If I did, I would be lying. The sessions widened and deepened the chasm growing between Cliff and me. There was no reprieve. The days with zero words spoken to one another increased, sexless days and nights piled up, and my mistrust toward Cliff extinguished any goodness left within me.

The ratchet couples counseling sessions with Neil became a landing place for me to release all the things that I had been holding back from yesterday or even from the two years before. I spent countless hours venting about Cliff and waiting on Neil's guidance to show up. As the sessions continued, Cliff began to open up more about his dissent and share his perspective about how our challenges were stemming from the baggage that I brought in.

"She's the one with all of the trauma. I have never experienced any trauma like that in my life. I don't have any trauma. She needs to fix the relationship with her dad; they haven't had a relationship since we've been together. I hate that she treats me like all the others that came before me. I've done none of the horrible things they've done, but it's like she's punishing me for what they did."

He didn't stop there. He drove his point home about how our situation was my doing, "She wanted all of this life. She wanted to buy the house and live above our means. Getting married was her idea. I told her several times how I felt about marriage. I wanted to make her happy, so I went along."

I had heard much of this before—most times discounting it as bullshit because it sounded like a cop out. The way he told it, he was the hero. He had taken his hands off the wheel while his body was still in the car (as I allegedly drove recklessly) because he'd do anything to please me.

What set me off during the sessions was his flat tone. He delivered these messages as punches without making eye contact. I could feel the satisfaction radiating from his body as I sobbed. His words became verbal jabs landing on my rib cage.

The whole world knew that I was walking around blindly without my mom and keenly aware of my tenuous relationship with my dad. Both of these situations made me feel tender, like an exposed nerve. Some things you just don't let others touch without permission.

I began to believe that he wanted to punish me for making him come here in the first place. For him, this wasn't about fixing anything. It was about proving to me that counseling didn't work and using his words to drive that point home.

I felt wronged by Cliff's behavior and how he gave Neil a front row seat to the madness. It felt like gooey mud was being slapped across my face as Cliff regurgitated the handful of secrets that I'd shared in solidarity with him about others that came before him.

Even as I was slowly becoming aware of my uncommunicated deep mistrust creeping into our relationship, I also managed to give credence to the invisible limits to how much harm Cliff could inflict. He wasn't a cheater, nor did he put his hands on me like others had. At least the physical scars fade over time.

There were other betrayals of the heart that hurt just as much, if not more—like the broken promises to fully carry his financial share of the bills that left me scraping to figure out a plan B or C. My stress levels would spike during these times, making it difficult to sleep at night. Unfortunately, subsequent discussions to handle things differently never really amounted to changed behavior. My cumulative bad experiences before and during my relationship with Cliff made me question my ability to ever feel steady and helped to intensify the brokenness and embarrassment that wouldn't let up.

Despite it all, I believed that I was doing all I could

to stuff that all in the basement in order to have a life with him—a life that he said he wanted and then conveniently changed his mind about. And yet, I still wanted to make things work and deeply loved the man that I'd met.

Confusion ran deep in my bones, making it hard for the love I held in my heart to be enough of a reason to stay.

I began questioning my desire and capacity to live in a loving, non-toxic household, where wonderful memories are made. A house where the kids were whole and could grow up with strong roots that leave their mark on the world. You know, the good kind.

To his credit, Cliff attempted to grab my attention to express how poorly our therapist was handling us and how nothing ever seemed to get resolved. We were only there to hurl insults at each other; there was no learning new tools or ways of being together. He was right in his observation, but my trust in him was virtually nonexistent. So, when these warnings came, they went ignored—until a light bulb went off for me.

Shot clock, I thought to myself in the midst of session five. Neil was out of his depth with us, and in that moment, we all realized it and were willing to acknowledge it at the same time. The clock had run out for him.

Neil suggested that maybe we each seek our own therapists. It honestly sounded like a hopeless suggestion at the time. But little did I know, it would become the license I needed to pursue looking backwards in my life to understand how I got here. It would be the nudge that would lead me to Lucia and the oceans of healing I would swim through in her witness.

By the end of our time with Neil, it wasn't just my heart that hurt—my body was crying for mercy. I had begun to notice the negative effects on my body with each session and could no longer deny how much it ached from being torn into shreds, no signs of restoration in sight.

All roads were leading to the need to look into why I was experiencing so much emotional and physical pain. I had to heal myself first.

The day after leaving Neil's office for the last time, I secretly quit my marriage.

Trying to fix it and myself at the same time felt like too much of an arduous task. The focus needed to be on me for now, and finding my own therapist would be my next best step in processing this experience and the ones before it. I desperately needed to know how I got here, with both feet sinking into quicksand.

CHAPTER 17:

Smacking the Pavement

My eyes glazed over as the flickering cursor blinked back at me. Three sentences sat on the screen like tired workers.

After what felt like an eternity lost in thought, my mind had become a tangled web of frustration and fatigue. There was a hollow pang tapping in my stomach as I fought the need to stop. Determination was moving through me like a stubborn blaze, urging me to push past the exhaustion and wrestle this chapter into completion.

Cliff peeked into the living room. "Maybe you should take a break to at least eat something," he offered gently. I could see the concern growing each time he entered, but I waved him off, my fingers steady on the keys, waiting for magic to appear.

The vision of wearing that cap and gown for my doctorate was within reach, a promise that I made to myself and my family. I could feel my mom's glowing admiration and unwavering support flowing from heaven. We had talked about this dream when she was still with me. I just needed to knuckle down by any means necessary—Malcolm's voice was blaring through a megaphone.

October was only a couple of weeks away. This time was always a marathon at work, each day packed with meetings and deadlines. My dissertation submission had to come before then if I wanted a fighting chance to make it through this fundraising season alive. Another year of toggling in between the two wasn't an option.

But my brain betrayed me, a once-reliable friend now hiding in the dark, each thought fading before I could grab it. Words dripped onto the page, sluggish and reluctant, as if they were ladled with molasses that refused to flow.

This brain of mine was usually my superpower, one I leaned on day in and day out. It got me out of jams with ease most times. When I was in the groove, my thoughts mirrored that of smooth, creamy peanut butter. There was no way I would ever get out of this program or succeed at my job or in life without it.

I sat on the couch for another hour, forcing out two more sentences, trying to pull something smart from the depths of my mind without success. My usual ritual of pacing felt futile; my thoughts remained stubbornly locked away, as if sealed behind a door that I had lost the keys to.

Steamy tears streamed down my face in response to the stale talent show playing out on my computer screen. There would be no amazing acts to see tonight. The trailers carrying the talent hadn't even pulled into the arena parking lot yet—for I was the main event, and so far I was failing miserably. Refunds for this lackluster performance were imminent.

I had never been here before. My brain had never just stopped working on me, especially in times of great pressure. Pressure typically fueled my fire. Pushing for and getting more had become a dangerous game that I craved to play.

"Good things come from pressure," I would always tell myself as I pushed and pushed. The deadlines got met, and the accolades poured in. I longed for the rush that came oozing down after another win.

That night, I was chasing an elusive high that never came, leaving behind the bitter aftertaste of an unmet goal. My self-imposed deadline floated right on by while I helplessly watched from the bench, head and shoulders slumped down in defeat.

This creator had been left for dead, and help was not on the way. I slammed my computer down in deep frustration as my vision started to blur and anger crept in. She and I had been in a nearly four-decade relationship by now, so when she showed up, I felt seen.

Usually, anger's arrival signaled a dark reunion.

Together, we'd dive into the shadows, swapping tales of betrayal and loss. We would discuss the nefarious things I'd done because of her temper, and our ensuing laughter would change the energy.

Retribution came easy when she was around. My body would jump into action—eyes turning into fiery lasers capable of setting anything that came into view aflame. Burning down everything around me was both a release from the internal heat and a balm for my insatiable ego. Only after the Earth was scorched could I move into the reconstruction period.

But tonight felt foreign. A restless energy simmered under my skin. I lacked the capacity to engage with her like old times, as I was still reeling from shock. My brain had been smashed into a thousand pieces, and after a brief period of painful silence, I was ready to have anger leave. We were never good at getting anything positive done together, if I was being honest. Burning evidence that could lead to solving this case wasn't presenting itself as a viable option. What I longed for that night was the focus needed to generate another win, something akin to the smell of bread baking in the oven. Displeased with my retreat, anger hissed at me like a black cat before slinking away.

A few days later, I pushed through the revolving door leading to Lucia's downtown office, my reflection in the glass revealing a half-done hairdo. My barely-put-together outfit hung on me like an afterthought, a testament to the battle fought to get there. Despite my disheveled state, relief swept over me as I walked in her door. I had honored a promise made during a dark time—to seek help and disentangle the web of mess I'd made. I was here, and I was doing the work.

Perhaps Lucia could pick the lock to the door with the lost keys. Was it possible to reclaim the clarity that had escaped me that now felt like a distant memory? Unsure about her ability to put Humpty Dumpty back together again, I reminded myself of the resolve I almost always felt in the days after our sessions.

Sunlight poured through the office windows between the adjacent skyscrapers, giving the space a toasty glow that danced across the yellow loveseat and ocean-blue chair. That chair had seen many of my trials—its commanding armrests high enough to hold any burden that I came to shed. Lucia's desk was a chaotic symphony of clutter. She had papers in several stacks, making productivity possible. It mirrored my own disarray, yet in some ways felt more purposeful.

As I settled onto the small couch, I could feel Lucia's

gaze, a blend of curiosity and concern. My heart raced, interpreting her quietness as a question. Was I wearing the chaos I felt inside?

"So, what do you want to talk about today?" she asked. Deep in my belly, I felt the words crawl up through my throat. Today, I needed extra time to string them together. How could I explain that my brain had become an old car alternator, giving out without prior warning? Tears welled in my eyes, making their appearance before my words did.

My body was cold and shaky, still experiencing the chill and distress from the other night. I could feel the exhaustion from the workday and the lack of sleep—my brain's remnants had struggled to shut down enough for sleep to take over. Instead, my subconscious flashed bright yellow and orange warning lights, signaling that something was terribly wrong.

The unfamiliarity of this experience unsettled me. I felt like a fragile piece of China moving about in a factory filled with knives and other sharp objects that could undo the fragmented pieces of tape holding what was left of myself together.

In the four short months of seeing her, much of our time together had been spent sorting through the treasure of secrets that had been sealed shut, only opened when new qualifying events needed refuge. Personally, I wanted to work through current events, the reasons that were wholly responsible for why I needed individual therapy at all. And because of this, Lucia had become well-versed in my many issues concerning Cliff and troubles at home.

She steered clear of judgment about Cliff, instead listening and using current events as a way into my past. She wanted in on the treasures buried at the bottom of the chest. Those treasures often required more support from Lucia to be unearthed.

I witnessed her masterfully observing my every move and mannerisms, checking for when my pregnant pauses filled the room or when my body began showing signs of remembrance. I would get tense and jerky—my legs shaking from side to side, my fingers fidgeting, every part of me working overtime to push out trapped, stagnant energy.

Our sessions were being threaded together, with Lucia asking probing questions from previous meetings, pushing me to dig deeper. "Tell me more about your childhood. How did it feel to be an only child? Getting all the cool toys made you feel good— what other things made you feel good? What kinds of things upset you?" Her tone conveyed curiosity; I could feel her zeal to learn and hear more about whatever I was trying so desperately to express.

Sometimes these old memories were easy to access. Closing my eyes helped me replay situations where my eyelids served as movie screens, tapping back into scenes of yesterday. I could even sometimes see what I was wearing, what the room smelled like, what was said.

One time, I was using this method in a session, and out of nowhere I recalled being assaulted at the age of sixteen by an older boyfriend named KC, at least five years my senior.

"Who is that in the background? You got somebody over there?" KC barked at me through the phone.

On this particular day, he had called and was angry about something. This was nothing new for our two-month affair. I wasn't alarmed by his harsh, sharp words, even though he sounded angrier than usual.

"Nigga, you crazy. There's nobody here. You're tripping," I responded.

He took a few deep breaths before speaking again, maybe trying to calm himself down. I interpreted this as a good sign. My body eased a bit until he spoke his next words, "You think someone is playing with you? I'm coming over. I'm going to beat your ass. I'm on my way now, and there better not be anyone over there."

KC slammed the phone down still screaming threats.

This flavor of wrath felt different. The butterflies in my belly started to rumble.

What in the entire fuck was about to happen? The way the call ended—KC was really coming—but there was no way he was coming to do what he said he would. Right? There was no way he was coming to hit me for something I hadn't done.

I exercised caution by calling Kia over to meet me outside, so that I wouldn't be alone when he pulled up. I was brief in my request to her. "KC is coming over, and he's talking big shit. I need you to come over in case some shit happens."

She arrived at my front door in T-minus five. We stood in the enclosed front door area with the mailboxes. In his fury, KC had clearly hijacked a jet to my house. He lived on the other side of town, and only fifteen minutes had passed before his car swerved on my block.

Walking up to the door, he seemed like his normal self. He even cracked a smile, which disarmed me enough to open the locked door as he motioned for me to do so. The three of us stood on separate walls, looking at each other with little dialogue exchanged. I was trying to size him up. Maybe he wasn't mad for real, or I had misheard his threat, and everything was okay. He continued to play it so cool that Kia made the decision to head home. Her friend was safe; the coast was clear.

As the door slammed behind Kia, the air thickened, and KC surged forward, the distance between us shrinking. Now standing about two feet away from me, he reached his hand up and back. I could see it moving toward my face in slow motion. I squeezed my eyes shut, bracing for the inevitable impact, my heart hammering like a frantic drum in my chest.

Instinct kicked in, and I twisted away, my body a coil of desperation as I fought to break free from his grasp and escape the suffocating hallway. With a swift motion, KC tore my shirt, his grip like iron as his fist connected with the back of my head, each blow a brutal punctuation to my cries for help.

"Help me! Help me, please!" I was in full sprint as I turned back into the alleyway to gauge how far I was from safety. KC was close on my heels, his eyes fixed with a determined look.

I made the fatal mistake of looking backward, which compromised my speed—so much so that KC was able to close the gap between us again, this time with a two-foot leap. I was running from a bionic leopard! The leap was enough to pummel me to the unforgiving ground, tangy blood exploding from my lips.

I covered my head with both arms as KC punched me over and over again. I just laid there; my spirit had left my body. The thumps kept coming, one by one. Each one erasing the pain from the preceding blow.

Somehow, the pain rolled backward, replaced by a numbness that flowed from my feet to the top of my head. The clock in my head had stopped ticking, and silence came over me. The alley had swallowed my screams—a void where help should have been—leaving me alone to face the storm.

I was just like that lady that had been beaten by those girls' father when I was a child. I remembered her, a shadow of a woman, surrendering beneath the heavy blows, her spirit, a ghost slipping away. I thought of a woman I had walked past a few months prior while visiting family in Times Square during spring break. A man had been beating her while she screamed, and no one had done anything, including me.

It took a moment for me to realize that the pounding had stopped and that KC had fled. I peeled myself off the pavement, looking around to confirm that I was indeed alone in the dark alley. Back in my body again, I immediately acknowledged that I ached all over. My head was throbbing like hell; it felt as if a wrecking ball were knocking down nerve-filled walls with a hammer. Both knees were scraped and bleeding. My shredded shirt was barely hanging from my torso.

KC said he was going to beat me up—and he did, I thought to myself as I walked up the stairs. I replayed the night's events, scanning for clues as to why I ended up battered. How in the actual fuck did this happen to me?

I was too embarrassed and scared to tell my mom about how I let this awful thing happen. Had I just told her, the situation could've ended with me having revenge for supper.

Lucia kept her focus on me as I relived this experience in her presence, only asking questions when I took pauses, attempts to fuse pieces of memory together.

"So, did you ever talk to him again?" she asked.

I shared how he called me some days later, asking if I was still mad at him. Disappointed by my affirming tone, he hung up on me. The slam of that hang-up was even harder than the one that had preceded the beatdown.

That hang-up would mark the end of KC and me. I never spoke to him again and did my best to forget him and erase what happened from my mind. At times I would be reminded by friends about the "guy who had jumped on my back," laughter erupting.

"So, you did share this incident with others. How did that go?" she asked.

"I regret telling anyone about it. What I wanted was pity, but it never came. Instead, I was met with laughter and disbelief before being cautioned to never see him again." Lucia's questions pushed me to unravel what happened before and after these types of situations. She did what she could to educate me about the purpose behind the work we were doing together. Traumatic experiences have a way of staying with you until you process them. Processing can take on many forms, but for me it involved first talking about them—letting someone in and learning the difference between hurtful experiences and traumatic ones.

According to Lucia, we all experience hurtful events—instances that cause pain and can knock us off kilter—but what happens on the other side of these events determines whether they have a lasting traumatic impact. What's most important is that we are open to, met with, or give ourselves support that helps us feel safe and confront the situation. In the absence of these things, the path forward looks different. When our body isn't given a chance to release the trauma, it creates long-term impact.

Traumatic events are not just situations that happen; they are continuous pain cycles that leave individuals with the burden of learning how to relate to others and themselves in a world that doesn't wholly respect or understand what healing looks like. What makes this even more difficult is that the pattern of trauma may be hard to spot because families can carry decades of painful memories that, if they remain untouched, have the potential to inflict harm on future generations—that is, until the disrupter shows up.

Through our discussions, she also helped to shed some light into how trauma manifests in the body. "Trauma is tricky. Things that you have buried and considered resolved may present themselves again and again," Lucia warned. "Your assessment of situations can be greatly altered after a traumatic event. And in your case, you have survived several instances of unresolved traumatic experiences."

Our work together helped to elevate the triggers left behind that served as unwelcome reminders—like Cliff trying to express intimacy by placing his hands near my neck, leading to my instinctive reaction of jumping out of my skin or angrily pushing him away.

"The accumulation of these occurrences has shrunk your capacity to think clearly. Your body has been in a constant state of fight or flight. The plan is to help you find and choose new ways of being that move your body and mind into a state that feels safe just for you."

Even in the early stages of exhuming my past piece by piece, we excavated bones that detailed my mom and dad's upbringing and their subsequent tumultuous relationship.

We talked through how my mom unsuccessfully tried to date after my dad, cutting men off at the knees after a handful of disappointments. She had learned to adhere to the depth of her tolerance for love and bullshit.

My dad, on the other hand, continued to date, even fathering another child after their lengthy courtship. Their varying paths forward created confusion, leaving me unsure of how to approach love in my own life.

It was those digging sessions that left my face drained of color, my clothes tattered, and my energy levels depleted. Saying that I was exhausted would be putting it lightly; the hanging battery in my back would need to be removed and placed on the charger for days. Sometimes longer charging periods were required to restore me to a level where I felt I could handle the mass of a gallon of milk using both hands.

My brain started to recognize this pattern of purging and needing to rest, retreating from others, and losing interest in things that typically brought me joy—like taking a midday Saturday nap, reading a good book, or hanging out with friends. This caused a seedling of concern, prompting me to question Lucia and her techniques, whether the work we were doing was helping or hurting.

In response, she said, "This shit is going to hurt more and more before any relief comes your way. I just ask that you remember why you came and stay committed to getting the answers to the many questions you are exploring. On the other side of the inquiry and work lie the answers."

"But I'm freefalling! Where is the bottom?" I asked several times. The thought of walking down creakier, winding, dusty stairs sent shivers down my spine. If working through the first treasure chest hurt like hell, a second chest was sure to kill me.

My "come to Jesus" session, the one right after my brain had conveniently stopped operating, wasn't about digging at all. I had clearly hit my face smack dab on the pavement, and Lucia was trying to assess the damage and determine what was needed to get my attention. She needed me to understand the severity of the situation before her hand would be forced to take on other, more extreme measures.

This session with Lucia resulted in a promise to take a sabbatical from work. She tried to get me to agree to put down my schoolwork too, which was a hard no for me. With all the chaos around me at work and home, school felt like the only thing I could control. That ball was in my court, and it was mine to bounce as I pleased.

I desperately needed a win, something to go my way. Plus, the window of completion was closing in on me fast. JD was working to complete his undergraduate degree in the spring, so finishing my own and getting out of the way was paramount. This masterful plan would help me dodge any conflicts with our ceremonies taking place on the same day or week. This was the only way, I told myself, even when Lucia tried her hardest to get me to see the other possibilities.

I promised to call my board chair on the train ride home to inform her of my plans to take a leave during the organization's busiest season. Lucia warned that if I didn't take the time off, the consequences would be far worse. The bottom I had been trying to gauge was here, and it would indeed consume me whole if I didn't respond in a healthy way. So, I begrudgingly agreed to take two and a half weeks off from work, focus on finishing my dissertation, and put everything aside until I returned from celebrating the six-year anniversary of my mom's death.

Our timed session had moved well past its end, but Lucia was still holding me hostage. She was seeking something more from me, and her disposition prompted me to make more promises to get ahead of the possibility of her making a dreadful call to have me committed. If that happened, what was left of my control would be snatched away, causing the barely visible China pieces to crash to the floor, melting into unrecognizable fragments, devoid of reassembly to convey the image I was trying so hard to show the world. I'd be finished and have to start anew.

Instead, I heeded her concern for my well-being and vowed to honor this break, figuring out how to confront all the contents of both treasure chests. This meant being willing to try things I'd never done before—no longer relying on my need to think through all the steps to achieve a new outcome, but trusting that the process would lead me to something better. I aimed to stay locked in on the vision and get to the other side.

Before leaving Lucia's office, I made a mega promise to slow down at the end of the year and reflect on my options for moving at a different pace in 2020. Finishing this degree and getting through this busy season would provide the right amount of appeasement for me to sit tight for a beat. This hurried pace over two decades had finally caught up with me, forcing me to confront the reality that my old ways of pushing were over (for now).

Her final words to close the session still ring in my head today, "Once you slow down for real and things feel stable, something interesting and scary may happen. Your brain will think that the time for resolution has come and will bring back things you've buried deep."

My time away from work gave me space to look at myself in the mirror—to notice the blemishes on my skin, the roundness of my belly making my pants tighter, and traces of hair thinning around my face. How did I miss all these changes in my appearance? I barely recognized myself or what was left of me.

The timing of my breakdown coincided with the anxiety bubbling in my belly daily, the increased nightmares of seeing my mom slip away in that hospice room, and the uptick in sad spells when the tears wouldn't let up.

I wasn't nearly as sad as I had been in previous years around this time, but the heaviness of her death began to cause body aches and produce flashing images of her lifeless face, even when I was awake. I hated how trauma worked to reduce my memories to this sad time. I kept reassuring myself that this, too, would pass and tried to remain grateful that I now had the words to explain what was happening in real time.

After finishing and submitting my dissertation chapters, I unplugged from school and work. My team was briefed on the plans and jumped into action to keep things moving in my absence. My return would occur about a week before our big gala. There was plenty to do, but the team assured me that taking care of myself and stepping back so they could stand in the gap was for the best.

On a whim, I bought a weekly pass at the local yoga center near my house. While I hadn't officially achieved yogi status, I was well aware of the benefits my body and mind experienced after every session over the years. Listening to my body, I slept a lot.

Taking midday naps became the norm, and most of the time I woke up feeling rested and ready to seek out the next adventure.

Similar to my time off between jobs years ago, I spent time with friends and continued planning excursions for my upcoming trip to Louisville. In that city, I would celebrate another year since my mom's passing.

The gala went off without a hitch, and I couldn't have been happier. I returned to work just in time to push outstanding, critical tasks over the finish line. My team held down the fort, providing reassurance in my decision to step back and only checking in to see how I was progressing.

JD and other family members attended the festive event. We danced, laughed hard, and raised money as a collective. Pictures capturing the joy we experienced that evening still make me smile. The drinks flowed well into the night as we kept the party going in my hotel room, with security coming several times to warn us to keep the noise down.

It was that night that I awoke to the terrifying dream of a younger me trying to catch myself. Here I was at the height of my professional and scholastic achievements, and still, that sad, desperate girl was chasing me. My break from work had been an important first step, but I realized that night that I still had a long way to go to heal that traumatized girl deep within me.

CHAPTER 18:

Tipping Point

I successfully defended my dissertation in November 2019. Saying that I was elated is an understatement. I was standing on Mount Kilimanjaro and ready to conquer the next one—graduation day.

The morning of graduation day started off shaky. As I made my face, my heart was in my mouth. My hands moved slowly, trying to fight off tears that were brewing.

Moments like these, I craved my mom's physical existence to experience the full range of feelings.

Talking to her helped to steady my hand, "Ma, can you believe that this day is here? I'm sure you can; you always saw the best in me. I need you today. Keep me nice and patient with the crowds. You know how I can get. Keep my spirits high and a smile across my face, please."

I had started talking to her more frequently to ease the distance between heaven and Earth. I've been known to walk the Target aisles and have full blown conversations with her, feeling her responses in the colors that catch my eyes, changes in the air, and music playing over the speaker.

Nearly thirty friends and family members attended the ceremony. The screams that erupted when my name was called drowned out the announcements of my fellow classmates. Standing on that stage, I devoured their cheers into my chest, hands over my mouth, tears slowly crawling down my face.

Cliff planned an incredible surprise party later that evening. My heart exploded when the crowd yelled, "Surprise!" as soon as my foot crossed the threshold. Genuinely startled by the sea of familiar faces waiting to hug and personally congratulate me, I needed a moment to take it all in.

Tears of happiness poured all night, like the many rounds of cocktails. I thought to myself, *This has to be what utopia feels like.* But I spoke too soon. Cliff took the surprise to another unimaginable level by unveiling a painting of my mom from a bright spot in our time together during her cancer fight.

During his unveiling speech, Cliff shared, "There was one person that I would've done anything to have here in person tonight, and this was my way of making that dream come true."

As soon as the sheet came off the painting, my knees buckled and the room went silent as my eyes locked onto the image. Her beautiful face filled the canvas. She was all made up with cleanly arched brows, bright red lips, blush accentuating her high cheekbones, and eyes gazing over her left shoulder at a bright orange and yellow monarch butterfly resting nearby. A turquoise background, with patches of white peeking through, framed her face.

Fixated on my mom's makeup, I lost all consideration for my own as I stood in the middle of the packed room.

A mudslide of mascara, shadow, and foundation crashed down my face as I was pulled into a nearby bathroom where a dear high school friend was waiting with her makeup kit to put me back together.

I danced until my shoes came off, cried until my ducts were empty, and laughed until my belly was sore. Now, this was the way to end a year!

I was ready for my slowdown in 2020, even if what it would look like wasn't entirely crystal clear. What I did know was that I had finally earned a break, I wanted more time for sleep, and I was prepared to welcome fun with my arms wide for anything that brought joy closer.

For me, that would include hanging out with Cliff and our younger sons and spending lots of time with my girlfriends in the streets. Maybe I would travel and create new memories in other cities. Cliff and I had dipped our toes in the international pond earlier in the year by traveling to Jamaica and had ended the year with our annual family vacation, this time in Cape Coral, Florida. Both trips ignited a passion in me to seek out more adventure, either in the States or elsewhere.

Doing more work wasn't on my mind at all. Overall, I felt content with the team and our focus on women's health at my current job. The once-turbulent tides there had calmed considerably. My confidence in my charge for what needed to be done there was at an all-time high.

Maybe this slowdown could help give space to dig deeper into why I was so absorbed with living a life on the go, dissecting that nightmare I had at the hotel after the gala. I could use this downtime to ponder the many ways my future life could look somewhat different from the one I had built that no longer served me.

I didn't have to wait long for different to come; 2020 came in hot. COVID-19 smacked us all in the face in the early months. This was not nearly the change I had been dreaming about. And yet, I tried to remain hopeful that things wouldn't take a turn for the ultimate worst.

Instead, I spent time making plans in my head about how great it would be not to worry about the hustle and bustle of being away from my family for ten hours each day. No more getting up at six, getting the boys to school, and commuting for more than an hour each way for work. We would all be safer within the confines of our homes until this thing boiled over. Cliff and I would have more time to do all the things that time never permitted us to do. I kept telling myself daily that I had everything I needed to manage the many facets of life while in my pajamas.

Less than a month into the pandemic, I received a non-disclosure agreement and a meeting invitation from executive leadership. On the call, I was informed that the organization was shifting focus, which meant that all of our jobs would be eliminated, though there might be another opportunity available for me.

I checked out after hearing the words, "We are going in another direction," and couldn't slam my laptop closed fast enough when the meeting ended. My thoughts were racing—the vision, the plan, the team, the culture, and everything I had worked so hard to build would be gone by the end of the year.

Before the call ended, I was reminded about the NDA and that this news needed to remain confidential until the green light was given. I felt stuck between a rock and a hard place, unable to escape the immediate connection I felt to all the loss spinning around me.

What I thought would only be a handful of weeks at

home turned into several months right before my eyes. I was in no way prepared to keep the ship going for that long, which led me to start doing things outside my norm. I went into full vigilante mode, watching millions of hours of news across several platforms. My thirst for information to help me wrap my mind around this hell became intense.

Before COVID, I only watched the news for the weather forecast to determine my outfit choices and mostly relied on trusted sources to tell me about the real happenings. Now, I was watching in real time and discussing with anyone who would listen about how the world was self-destructing. This absorption and release of information quickly turned into an obsession, birthing more angst in my heart by the minute. Even with this realization, I couldn't turn off the TV or social media.

I was mindlessly scrolling late one night when the video of George Floyd being murdered by the Minneapolis police came across the screen. My eyes filled with tears as he screamed for his life—calling for his mother to come to his aid. It was this cry for help that ripped open the scab holding my own heart together as a Black mother of three Black boys in this country.

Before watching the video, I had buried the pain and fear of my own children meeting the same fate. Seeing this atrocious act reminded me of a call from a then-fifteen-year-old JD in 2013 when the Zimmerman verdict was released after he had murdered Trayvon Martin. We had intently watched the trial together, rationalizing what had seemed to us an open-and-shut, guilt-ridden case.

"Ma, what does this mean for me? Ma?" the cracked

voice on the line asked. My baby was pleading with a mom who had no answers and only fear in her heart.

Seven years had passed since then, and numerous Black men and women had lost their lives at the hands of police. The murders of Breonna Taylor and George Floyd in 2020 enraged a subset of the world as we were losing hundreds of thousands of lives to COVID. Collectively, we were reminded of what it meant to be Black in America.

The once-cool term "sheltering in place" now carried a new meaning that looked more like protests to humanize Black lives, clearing out store inventories and hoarding essentials, misinformation spreading like wildfire, strangers fighting over social media, and prolonged periods of physical disconnection from loved ones. The chaos outdoors made it difficult to not confront whatever troubles had been lurking behind my own walls.

Having the boys home twenty-four seven during the first few weeks felt like a gift. We ate breakfast slowly and together most mornings. I enjoyed the many hugs I received while walking past them on my way to the bathroom. I relished the many chances to hear them giggle more and listen to what they learned at school over dinner. Our old ways of living had never afforded us this time.

After getting them settled on their laptops for school, Cliff and I retreated to our offices to do what work we could until they needed something or a break in our schedules arose. Some school days, our routine worked like magic;

many others, it was a madhouse. One day, I excused myself from a Zoom call because I heard scuffling in the kitchen, which doubled as a school cafeteria and classroom. Walking into the room, I saw both boys rolling around on the floor. The culprit that caused the ruckus was an eraser.

I was already fading from the inside before receiving the news that JD's graduation ceremony was canceled and would instead be a YouTube video. Waking up most mornings exhausted, moody, and with a soaked pillow became my norm.

This was not like me; I could always find the words to tell my story, even just a little. Instead, I started making up reasons and ways to create a narrative. Maybe I needed to go to bed earlier or have a nightcap cocktail to knock me out. Oh wait, maybe I needed to host another Zoom meetup or dinner in the freezing cold with my homegirls. Unfortunately, I would follow through on these plans without experiencing any improvement.

Cliff tried to point out how I was changing, but to no avail. His words fell on deaf ears. He'd beg me to talk to him using different techniques, like giving examples of how I had changed or hurling questions my way to get my attention. "Babe, something is up with you; you seem really irritable lately. This is more than usual. Have you noticed? Have you talked to Lucia about what's going on?"

In return, I would respond, "Yeah, I've noticed. I'm doing what I can. Shit is just bad for everyone right now. Leave me alone." I purposely pushed away his attempts to connect—I was convinced that they were meant to distract me from what I was feeling in my heart about our marriage. I wanted to leave and escape out the back door, leaving no trace that could lead to my whereabouts.

Lucia did what she could to help me focus our

weekly sessions on small wins. "What are the things that make you feel good? How often are you able to make these things happen? Who or what do you need to feel good?" This line of questioning brought enough light to reveal how much my health had deteriorated.

The many consecutive days of wearing yoga pants disguised my growing waistline and the increase in the scale's digits. My skin had started to look flaky, and I was wearing pimples longer than I was used to.

My resentment toward Cliff had grown immensely before COVID, and now here we were, spending nearly every waking minute together. What a gift. We were caught in a vicious cycle, with many good days followed by too many bad days of arguing and tone-deaf silence.

Our arguments were about the same issues from yesterday's past—him being upset with me for not prioritizing his need for connection and my relentless pursuit of collective success and prosperity. The promises for a beautiful life together had gone unfulfilled, and it was all his fault. I was keeping my end of the bargain by staying focused on flourishing professionally and ensuring we had what we needed financially to keep us all afloat.

Nearly all of my therapy sessions had become consumed by the many ways I felt Cliff was ruining my life. Why couldn't he show up the way he had said he would?

Some answers came our way when Cliff decided to seek individual therapy from a pastor who officiated his friend's wedding. He found himself moved by Pastor Freddie's perspective on marriage being joy-filled and the importance of both minds and boats rowing in the same direction.

Encouraged by Cliff 's openness toward therapy and his consistency with virtual visits, I accepted the invitation to join him and Pastor Freddie sometimes.

I instantly found something special and calming about the way this middle-aged white man was able to empathize with Cliff and me. In our first session together, he jumped right in, "So tell me about yourself. What has happened that hurt you? Share only what feels comfortable to you."

Thankfully, I had some experience learning how to share my story as part of my visits with Lucia, as well as giving Cliff snippets here and there. *All I have to do is be brave and do it again,* I thought to myself.

Flinging myself right into the deep end, I shared how I had been raped multiple times, about my troubled relationship with my dad and his addiction, and how betrayed I felt by Cliff 's actions in not being the man he said he would be to me. Pushing through tears, I expressed my exhaustion from all this suffering and the realization that sustained happiness didn't exist here. Maybe it never did.

Pastor Freddie listened intently, looking directly into my eyes and soul with compassion before sharing the gifts he had neatly tucked into his pocket. His wife had also experienced similar hurts, like abuse, and had worked through the pain over time. Lots of therapy, taking steps forward and backward, and growing closer to each other was a critical part of her healing. He openly acknowledged causing pain to his wife and the need to deal with his own trauma before being able to support her.

To him, my situation revolved around two things— my inability to enjoy what was in front of me and the narrative I had created about life getting in the way of my success. He asked, "What do you need to do to enjoy life?" and "What do you need to do in order to move closer to Cliff?" In the latter question, he was direct with his word choices—clarifying that he didn't want to know how I thought I could move forward, but rather toward.

My mind drew a blank, and I realized these two questions deserved reflection. I was struck by the agency in his questions—he was placing the ball back in my court.

And he didn't stop there. According to him, the situation with my dad was in desperate need of some shifts, as well. He suggested that I start thinking about my dad more as a friend than a parent. Because of my dad's addiction, I couldn't rely on him to behave in ways I believed a father should. But maybe if I saw him as a friend and created a healthy list of expectations of him, our dynamic could change.

The pile of Kleenex in front of me was a solid gold representation of the soul purging that took place that day, leaving me with questions to reflect on. Had the time come for me to stop only sharing the awful things that had happened to me in this life? Could I really accept all the terrible choices I had made that had landed me in this quagmire?

In the months to come, I spent subsequent sessions with Lucia and Pastor Freddie, dialoguing about what steps could be taken, which often illuminated more questions. What does a joy-filled marriage look like? And how could Cliff and I reframe the friendship in our marriage?

The time between sessions allowed me to contemplate the endless possibilities that hadn't presented themselves before. These possibilities kept returning to one thing and one thing only—in order for me to feel good in my relationship with Cliff, I needed to feel good about the one I had with myself.

Zoloft was prescribed in the early fall to manage the anxiety and depression diagnosis that I had received after a couple of visits with my doctor. "You won't feel better quickly; you will need at least three months before something happens," she cautioned.

I was blessed when the placebo effect quickly took hold in my mind. With every pill consumed, I told myself that I was making things better by knowing that help was on the way.

The countless hours of TV watching didn't entirely go to waste because the Peloton commercials turned me into a new customer. Before COVID, I had never been a gym-goer nor held a membership—it felt too much like a commitment I was never ready to make. There was an instant love connection with the instructors and their stories. I took baby steps by attending a couple of cycling classes a week, increasing my attendance as the weeks progressed. Then I moved into other wellness options like meditation, Pilates, and weight training.

I secretly made a promise to myself to take classes at least three times a week and see what happened. The sense of community I felt with other virtual class attendees, along with classes taken with friends who also owned bikes, was a strong motivator for keeping this promise and enjoying the process.

In the eight months after COVID touched down, I began to take note of a newer version of myself emerging. All I had to do was spend a few moments prioritizing at least one thing that made me smile. On some days, it was that spin class that left me breathless, and on others, it was the stroll around the block with Cliff and the boys to talk about the day.

Cliff started to show improvements in his ability to communicate how he was feeling on any given day and was actively working with the pastor. He was on his path to learning how to unpack his own past and understand its implications for our relationship. Hope was rearing its head in my heart again; maybe Cliff and I were capable of turning this ship around for the better.

This girl was learning how to be a woman taking charge of her needs and life. An active job search for a new role ended with me turning down three jobs and making the decision to launch my own consulting practice.

All of the uncertainty brought on by the pandemic had helped forecast what my future could hold—one that wasn't entirely dependent on my old ways of being. A journal entry from that time read:

> *My knowing woke me up this morning as my soul rejoiced. I NEEDED this shift in my life—I needed to shake things up to create life-changing moments in the now, not tomorrow and not next year. The pandemic, the consolidation at my job, my mental growth—all had to happen for me to get here. My 'here' has me so excited and willing to jump in headfirst into my near and distant future.*

I could feel the chains of old habits breaking and an increasing need to soak up every moment of life through work, social activities, and other pastimes. There was one new requirement—spending my time doing things that matter to me. The focus for me was to create more freedom so that I could fully bask in the liberties that I knew were coming—being with my boys, leaning into my relationship with Cliff, growing together and not in silos.

The fear of the unknown had dissipated; it wasn't gone. Instead, I was learning how to change my relationship with fear and use it for the purpose of fueling the journey ahead. I could now acknowledge when it came and bust through it.

PART 4:

Flying

CHAPTER 19:

A Winding Staircase

Feelings of hopefulness didn't last nearly as long as I'd expected. A nagging sensation crept into my gut, planting the seed that there was more to be done to overcome this mountain of pain that had somewhat eased and then returned with a vengeance.

I'd learned about reiki healing from a friend who had experienced a session. I was immediately curious and booked the next available appointment. The idea that energies could be released from the body without the conscious mind having to work so hard appealed to me. I was ready to allow healing work to be done *through* me instead of *by* me. Plus, I was still trying to address this physical and emotional pain that seemed to have me in a chokehold.

"The theme for your session is restorative healing. You are tired, but not old Negro spiritual tired—just day-to-day tired," said Kasey, the reiki healer.

"I can see that you've been out here showing up as an external version of yourself, but the internal version requires some healing," she continued.

"Throughout the entire reading, I tried to get you to come out, but without any success. There was a

185

little girl version of you hiding; something has hurt you deeply, and there's sadness tucked away inside. It's time to deal with it. Your throat chakra spoke the loudest to me; you have things to say but haven't. Is any of this resonating with you?" She paused for a brief moment.

The tears had already begun to fall. My stomach clenched from the anguish of being discovered, despite my efforts to hide somewhere safe in the bushes. There was no ambush, just words of wisdom flowing from her mouth to my ears.

I was unable to speak, so she continued, helping to break up the silence, "You are operating out of alignment. There are parts of you hiding that you don't want people to know. There's a disconnect between the little girl hiding and the woman presenting herself to the world."

I interrupted, "I'm scared. My mom died. She was the strongest person I've ever known, and she was taken away within four months. My brain still hasn't been able to wrap around what happened. I feel like an orphan who doesn't know what to do or who to be, or whether I will ever be anything without her. The brevity of her passing created an urgency in how I've chosen to live.

"Whatever it is that I think I want to do, I do it. I'm scared of dying. I have three boys and don't want to leave them here alone. My husband is a great guy, but I don't know if I will ever reach my potential with him.

"I've been going to therapy for some time and have worked to share some pretty awful things with her, and even with Cliff. I just feel stuck—even though progress is being made.

"I believe that the next step for me is much bigger,

but I can't see anything. I think fundamental to all of this is figuring out how to feel whole. And this is why I'm here."

There, I had shared my deepest fears with someone I'd just met. My voice was shaky as I pushed out thoughts that were scrambled in my mind. I had gotten somewhat used to sharing parts of myself with Lucia over the last three years, but this experience caught me off guard.

Kasey listened as I spoke, giving me the sense that she understood both ends of the tension—the discombobulated internal side, highly stunted by the passing of my mother, and the egotistical external side that wanted to show the world I had what it took to still live without my mom. I was broken, but I wasn't going to let this truth break me.

Kasey was able to see me without truly seeing me. To her, I was a little girl hiding, pretending to be an adult in a world that had scarred and maimed me. Her words stung not because they were untrue, but quite the opposite—her reading was spot on.

I was fearful and masking this truth. My zest to live fully was being driven by the fear residing in my heart—fear buried so deep, untapped and guarded by tripwires that, when touched, set me off into an angry response. The walls I'd built around this fear made it virtually impossible for me to access it, so instead, I tried to ignore its existence, praying it would go away by moving forward with the many plans I'd set forth to live the life I've always wanted.

I was fearful of anything and everything. What if I were to leave my boys before they were ready for me to do so? What if this cruel world snatched one of them from me? That reality would surely be the end of me.

I'd been impatiently holding my breath, waiting for the news about when Cinco would need to have that dreaded heart surgery to fix the abnormality the doctors told us about ten years ago. Every year, we'd undergone testing and received news to wait another year. When would that other shoe finally drop? Could I survive another hospital stay with my baby as the patient? He had already been through enough. Could my marriage even survive this?

Two years in, therapy hadn't demonstrated how this tucked-away fear was controlling my being and the image of myself that I was putting out into the world.

Interrupting my thoughts, Kasey piped in, "It's time for you to heal the parts of you that couldn't fully grow up because of your mom's death. When a parent dies, it's a rite of passage that you haven't accepted. You aren't aligned with what's next for you."

She continued, "I can see the disconnect you are experiencing at home, but it appears to largely stem from you. You've been doing the work to let things out, but the healing has yet to start. You are still working through things; I get it. I want to encourage you to focus on maturing the emotional parts of yourself. I can see that you get angry quickly and that your breathing is short and shallow. This is because your nervous system isn't aligned."

I interjected with a chuckle, "I don't get angry quickly; I'm just easily agitated."

This woman was reading me with a magnifying glass, leaving no stone unturned. I couldn't leave without gaining some insights into how to unpack all that she had shared with me. The rational parts of my brain were craving something concrete to take home.

She emphasized the importance of continuing my self-care routine — working out, attending therapy, and engaging in other modes of well-being, like getting massages to calm and regulate my nervous system. My body needed more consistent signs that the danger had passed, no more fight or flight. I was safe — safe enough to come out from hiding and truly begin the work of healing my soul.

She also stressed that there were parts of me that didn't feel fully nurtured, and it was important to let others in to help care for me. She encouraged me to spend some time reflecting on how I want to be mothered in this next chapter of my life. I needed to dig deep and consider how to replace my mom in this role. Doing so would help me find the community I needed. Right now, the woman with maternal energy couldn't find me because I was still hiding and operating as the younger version of myself.

As Kasey put it, "You need this woman to nurture the adult version of you because your mother has already done the mothering of little you — that work is done."

The tears were still falling as we hugged at the end of the session. I continued to feel her wisdom during the silent ride home, replaying her words in my mind, "You are hiding from the world. You are presenting as a woman but operating as a child who has been deeply hurt."

There was so much clarity in her reading. I had been deeply hurt and was still experiencing pain that I had worked so hard to shield myself from. I felt better with this new layer of understanding, but at the same time, I could feel the ever-circling staircase of healing calling me forward. If there was anything I had learned from my journey thus far, it was that there was always another level, another layer to peel back and explore.

I told myself, "One more step, Harper. Just one breath after the next."

I knew I had it in me.

CHAPTER 20:

A Different Lens

My efforts to escape and let time ease my agony weren't working; the truths I'd uncovered in the reiki session with Kasey deserved more reflection.

I leaned on my sessions with Lucia to unpack the next layers. We talked through much of the painful past—the domestic violence I witnessed at an early age and my experience as a survivor in my teenage years. The discussions about the rapes were in great detail and spanned several sessions, focusing on the gut-wrenching pain they caused then and how these situations manifest in my life today.

Lucia continued to push me forward with her questioning, placing her foot in any door I cracked open. Whenever a glimpse of light crept in the hallway, she seized the opportunity to prop the door open wider, holding my sweaty hand as we made our way along the uncharted path back in time. One foot in front of the other, sometimes an inch shuffle forward was all I could muster, and that seemed enough for her.

Asking for more looked like her asking, "So how did that situation make you feel?" From time to time, she tried on words—measuring my responses for resonance or rejection.

Wrinkles formed between my brows as I struggled to find words to capture how I felt. I had never truly considered or examined my feelings in times of agony, making this challenge more difficult. My focus was always on the facts, and feelings were not facts.

Angry and sad were my commonly used synonyms to capture feelings. Those words seemed to sum up most situations nicely, with a pink bow. Several layers beneath the surface lay scarcity, unrelenting angst about the future, and disappointment in others and myself. Self-imposed feelings of guilt, shame, and regret lay bare on the treasure chest floor, abandoned for something stronger, like armor.

To me, these feelings were the cause of my straying so far from logic and diving headfirst into unsafe situations one after another. Caring about others and placing their needs and perceptions of who I was or wasn't above my own had gotten me into serious trouble. When I led with logic and things still went awry, I could intellectualize the situation and move forward more quickly.

Feelings felt foreign and risky at best. And yet, they were everywhere—in the movies I loved to watch, in the songs I loved to sing incessantly. Feelings were like lines etched into a record, playing the same tune nonstop. They made situations murky, harder to dissect and rendered facts increasingly difficult to piece together. At some point in life, I decided to put them aside, only facing them when they reared their ugly heads without my permission, when the ear-ringing explosion from a bomb I set off grabbed my attention.

Lucia, unbothered by my inability to attach feelings

to difficult situations, continued to encourage me to practice. She asked me to journal about instances that angered me and to sit with the discomfort I experienced, pulling in words to describe how my body felt, the thoughts running through my mind, and the actions I took. To this day, I'm still working hard to bring feelings into my world and can now see how critical it was to highlight the path of exploring my choices—or lack thereof—when these hurtful occurrences entered my life.

Admittedly, I would get frustrated with Lucia when she would ask how I might have contributed to these situations through my choices. Like, what the hell? I took her questioning as an attack on my character. Was she blaming me? I was already carrying busloads of shame and guilt, wearing a cloak to hide my face. Was coming here for help a bad idea? How was any of this connected to being my fault?

Sensing my distress and my retreat from these "blaming" discussions, Lucia instead tried to use my choice of Cliff as a partner as an example for exploring my decisions. She encouraged me to examine what elements of that story resulted from actions I took—like choosing to go out to dinner with my friend to meet someone new even when I knew my heart was still in pain from the previous relationship. What about my choice to keep calling and chasing Cliff during those periods when he was actively creating distance between us? Why had I been so determined to make the relationship work, even when it was showing signs of fissures early on?

Stepping back from these instances and examining both the micro and macro decisions helped me release some of my attachment to the narratives I had been telling myself. Instead, I began to get curious about other factors that had been left out of my accounts, prompting me to question my perspective. If other factors might have played a role but were left unaccounted for, perhaps my conclusions and how I was seeing things could possibly be flawed too. How might the outcome shift if these pieces were added retrospectively?

Crucial to this process was also the need to better understand how and why these stories controlled my narrative about life and relationships. How were they serving or harming me today?

I had been telling myself that Cliff chose this life and had plenty of free will to move on if he couldn't be who I needed him to be, or if he couldn't pretend to be the man I wanted him to be. Finger-pointing at each other had become our game, without an obvious end in sight. We bounced blame back and forth without acknowledging our own actions. I wasn't entirely blameless, but my empathy for him was nonexistent.

The man I had fallen in love with and chosen to build a life with had switched gears midstream without notice, starting to mirror the men from my past who had wronged me and gotten away with it. In the process, he, too, had scarred my heart and worked to cement my tainted belief in men. The embarrassment I felt inside created an internal conflict. I couldn't understand how I had seemingly chosen a different partner this time, yet the outcome was the same. Maybe it was me. Perhaps it wasn't that our relationship was broken but, rather, that I was. My inability to speak about the traumas of the past without feeling shame hindered my ability to confront them. I grappled with how I had chosen toxic partners time and again. How does that happen to a person who isn't also toxic?

Lucia aided in me backing things up a bit by helping to talk through my relationship with my dad in great depth and its connection to my relationship with Cliff. I spent hours sharing how my dad and I related to each other when I was a little girl, detailing my unmet needs and chronic disappointment in him. This exploration highlighted a gap in my need to fast-forward into forgiving him because I only had one parent left. My mom would have wanted me to forgive him too—just like she had before she left.

But how could I make peace with the past we both created by myself? My logical brain kicked into high gear. Not only was that unfair, but it was also terribly erroneous. I wasn't a fan of letting him off the hook, even though I held some sympathy for the addiction that held his executive function captive. It wasn't enough. I needed something more tangible to help me grasp the benefit. What would truly be in it for me to let go?

To me, letting go meant letting him off scot-free. My mom was a different woman than I was, and I could live with that for now. I didn't have to define myself by her ability to forgive him. The limited interactions between my dad and me left me feeling empty and sad. He was always pushing me to show him love and deference because he was my dad.

Somehow, I missed the crucial step of processing what happened to little me, which could partially explain why forgiving him simply because he was my dad and responsible for my existence just didn't sit right with me. My inner little girl craved acknowlededgment from him of how he had messed up and hurt her in the process. Lucia often asked what I would do if this reckoning never came. What else did I need; what could I do for myself to provide some closure?

To that, I held no answers.

Images from the hotel dream began flashing back. The terror in the eyes of my younger self was palpable. That girl had seen and endured the unthinkable, and the adult version of me was running from her because acknowledging her existence would topple the house of cards that I had feverishly built with sweat, tears, and bright red blood.

Knocking down that house meant I had to accept situations that couldn't be changed, taking the good and the bad at face value, and acknowledging the choices I had made that created the hell I was living in.

No matter how difficult that would be, the call to action was to stand in the sun and recognize that the little girl did the best she could with what she had. From there, maybe I could release the contempt I held for her, nestled in my adult heart.

Before I could do that, could I first confess how irate I was with her choices and how she allowed people to walk all over her? She kept returning to the fire after people had shown who they were time and time again. That girl wanted to see the good in others but lacked the ability to see any in herself.

I was embarrassed that she was a part of me. This contempt ran deep and would require new tools if this was what I wanted. I had two choices—keep running and hurting myself and others or detach myself from the beliefs and behaviors that led me here and do something different.

And doing something different was within reach. If I could level with myself, I could see that I was starting to feel a bit more in control of how I responded to challenging events when they came my way. Anger wasn't always the first emotion oozing out of me. When she did show up, I could keep our interactions brief and meaningful.

Whether I liked it or not, she showed up to teach me something, to alert me when my hand was on the hot stove. The onus was on me to receive the alert and remove my hand to reveal any emotions concealed by anger. I could then ask myself what else was there—was I also sad, annoyed, frustrated?

I had learned that emotions were more expansive in nature than the credit I had given them. Instead of repressing them and then burning down everything in sight, there was another way. I could articulate whatever was manifesting inside and around me, forming words to explain occurrences with a purpose defined by me. Sometimes I needed to use words to express myself; other times, those words led to solutions that may or may not result in action. Inaction observed by others didn't necessarily mean that nothing was being done. I had learned to release that mandate too.

Gratitude had finally received an invitation to my party—a party where I could start to feel expansion when I talked about the hurtful times. I was grateful for the ability to share these instances with others without diverting my eyes from theirs or letting my thoughts scurry away with my sanity, simultaneously filling my head with projections of my own insecurities about how they would see me after this. Sharing my truth was about releasing and doing what Lucia and Kasey said I needed to do—let people in.

I began to witness how my attachment to painful moments shifted. I wasn't those situations. This perspective shift allowed me to move away from the shame and guilt that covered my entire being and move toward openness and empathy for the woman I was today.

But something within me was still holding out this level of kindness for the little girl who needed me to see and honor her. Knowing that she needed me wasn't enough. My soul remained persistent, keeping me awake some nights or waking me up. There was an internal knowing that there was more for me to experience.

What started as a nudge transitioned into a consuming thought while sitting in work meetings or engaging in activities that brought me joy. The phrase "keep seeking" kept coming up and wouldn't let go.

Curiosity began to set in, putting me on a path of exploring alternative methods with proven benefits for healing trauma survivors. The universe has a way of sending signals once you open yourself up to possibilities.

CHAPTER 21:

Dream HER

"Hey, I heard you were looking for me," said the voice on the other end of the line.

I had stepped out of a conference meeting to take a call from an unknown number, something I don't typically do. "Hello?" I said again, curiosity lacing my voice.

"This is Diane."

I could feel a giddiness building in my belly. It had been nine years since my mom's service and since she'd uttered those fateful words—Call me when you are ready to talk.

Back then, I had nodded my head with a half-hearted yes. Today, feeling a bit stronger, I was somewhat ready to hear what she had to share about the hours of phone calls she had with my mom.

I had called Auntie a few days earlier to see if she could find Diane's number and pass it along to me. In the end, she called around and sent it via text. Even with the number in my hands, I still hadn't picked up the phone "Hi, Diane," I began. "It's so good to hear from you. And yes, I've been asking about you," I said.

An overwhelming feeling washed over my body,

and I smiled. It felt like my mom was right there, like she had told her to call me, perhaps knowing the time had come to receive a message.

"I want to learn about the conversations you had with my mom." Diane's remembrance-filled giggle came through the line, easing my shoulders as I waited for her to speak. "Oh yes, yes. Your mom and I had many conversations. I miss my friend. She loved you so much; I need you to know that. Our calls were about preparing her for her transition.

Your mom knew she was leaving and wanted to discuss what she needed to do to get ready. When we first started our talks, she was most concerned about ensuring that you and the boys would be okay with her release."

Diane continued as I listened, tears surging down my face in the empty parking lot.

"I coached her on first being okay with leaving. Your mom was tired, Harper. The pain in her body had become too much, and she had grown weary of it, especially knowing she had moved past the point of ever being healthy again."

"So, we spent a lot of time crying together, praying together, and preparing her soul to accept the decision to leave her body. It was only after she could accept this plan for her life that she could begin to tackle her feelings about making sure you could indeed release her when the time came.

"She didn't want to let you all down, H. There was something in her that knew you would never be ready to let her go."

Congestion began to build in my chest from the tears. I had to blow my nose several times even after the tears had stopped. All this time, I had been wondering how my mom was so ready to go when the answer had been here all along—she had been quietly crafting her goodbyes, stitching together memories and farewells, all while I remained focused on her staying, unaware of the preparations she had woven.

Sharing this insight with Diane provided more clarity. "Yes, your mom was ready and needed you to be brave and let her move on. Her work was done, babe. She told me many times that she knew you would be okay after she left, but her true concerns revolved around how you would respond to the heavy burden of letting her go."

Memories of discussions I had with my mom about miracles before she died started to flood my mind. When I wasn't begging God to save her, I was lying on her bed, talking about how He was going to save her just like He did with Cinco. Miracles were real to me because of how Cinco came into this world. If God could do that, He could indeed do it again with her.

Looking back, my mom would listen to my cries for a miracle but never gave me any sign of agreement. Perhaps she had been preoccupied with shielding her own feelings about the real plan and how I was feeding into her worries about my capacity to release her.

I told Diane about the hospital experience and how my mom was transitioned to hospice and how I let her go twice. Nine years later, I still can't explain how I did that, especially given all the things I had done to keep her here.

Diane shouted, "You gave your mom a wonderful gift, babe! You gave her what she needed. I'm proud of you. This is the gift that we will all want when our time comes, knowing that our loved ones are okay with us leaving."

Before ending the call, I let Diane in on something that occurred a few nights ago.

"I think my mom came to visit me the other day while I was talking on the phone with one of her sisters.

"I was standing at the kitchen counter rolling dough—preparing my mom's signature peach cobbler—when a cool breeze that chilled my body preceded a bright orange and red flash of light that zapped past me."

"I could only catch a glimpse of it through the corner of my left eye. It scared me. So much so that I didn't mention it to my aunt."

Diane cut in, "Babe, that's not your mom. Those are called unfamiliar spirits. God would never send your mom to you that way—she will visit you in your dreams."

"There will be no fear, babe. You and your mom were too close for you to be scared when she comes. I will say this too—when she comes, you will know."

We ended the call with plans to keep in touch. Standing in that parking lot with a tear-streaked face, I had been given a wonderful gift.

This call opened the floodgates to more memories and anticipation of the day when my mom would visit. Work would need to wait. I informed my client that I needed to leave for the day.

Diane was right about so much. I started reflecting on the dozens of dreams I'd experienced (and somehow forgotten) when my maternal grandmother died in 2007. The dreams were of us carrying on as we did in the physical world, spending our time gossiping about the family—like who had gained weight and who was dating who.

The laughter was nonstop; her happiness was

contagious. She was pleased to be with me, as I was with her. Sometimes we would sit in silence, painting each other's nails pretty hues of red.

I welcomed these dreams in the beginning, awakening with a smile on my face most mornings. They gave me the reassurance I needed to know that she held no grudges against me for not being by her side when she took her last breath, despite my attempts to make it.

For the six months leading up to her passing, I had devoted two weekends out of the month to making the four-hour drive to spend time with her. My aunt had called early that morning to tell me that the time was nearing. Still with us, my grandmother groaned in the background until my aunt put the phone to her ear.

"We are coming today. I promise," I said. They were my last words to her.

I tried many times to gather my family to make the four-hour trip, but ultimately, we didn't make it in time. My grandmother's body was cold to the touch by the time I walked into her bedroom. A lamp on the bedside table offered just enough light to capture the mix of emotions swirling throughout my body.

Crawling into bed, I wrapped my arms around her and professed my love and the trials that had gotten in the way of being with her as she moved on to the other side. My promise to be with her that day had been foiled, and for that reason, I wept.

I was angry and frustrated, and the dreams comforted me after the disappointment of that day. Until one morning I awakened with sweaty sheets and anger in my heart, and I knew they weren't serving me anymore.

"I need you to stop coming!" I pleaded. "I will never feel better if you keep coming."

Out of the blue, the dreams stopped, and I was relieved. Fast forward to fifteen years later when I woke up one summer morning with a wet pillow. Eyes closed, unceasing tears overwhelmed me as I pulled myself into an upright position to face Cliff, who was sleeping beside me.

An angelic grin formed on my lips as I whispered the words, "She's well."

Pausing for a second, Cliff turned from his side to face me before springing his body up to meet mine. I couldn't hold the words in any longer and jumped into recounting the details of my dream.

"She had silver-streaked hair that cascaded gracefully down her back, each strand catching the light like a crown, exuding an air of dignity that made my heart swell with admiration.

"Her frame was thin and short, fitting her body perfectly. I was struck by her exquisite facial bone structure from several feet away. This woman was stunning and confident in every way.

"As she moved closer, her light and warmth flowed toward me. I was in utter awe of her sheer white gown, which reflected light upon her hair and beautifully kissed skin. Her essence felt familiar as she walked in my direction.

"The space between us was beginning to slowly close, measured by the ticking of seconds. Then, like a jolt of electricity, recognition pulsed through my body. The familiar arch of her brow, the gentle curve of her smile—they pulled me back through years, each detail a thread waking up my senses.

"Her figure was just as I remembered it—perfectly

aligned with the way God made her sixty-eight years ago. Her glowing, radiant skin came into view, bouncing light back my way. God had restored her. This woman had shed the physical shell that weighed her down on Earth and seemed to float as she drew closer and closer.

"Her dark brown eyes were transfixed upon mine. I could see the rays of light expanding and illuminating the pathway between us. I remembered those eyes. Today, they were soft and welcoming. I drank them in as I opened my arms to greet her. Her arms reached outward too, wide and ready.

"When our bodies finally met, a rush of warmth enveloped me, like honey poured over a hot biscuit, filling the hollow spaces where loneliness had lingered. In that moment, the world outside faded. It was just us, coated in everlasting love—the kind that never leaves.

"I had been given another chance to hug my mom and couldn't resist the desire to melt into her arms and hold tightly. It was her.

"The familiarity of her touch zinged throughout every cell of my body. Another hug, I thought to myself. The embrace was kindred, as though no time had passed us by. She had never let me go since the last hug nine years ago; her arms had been wrapped around me all along.

"It was only after closing out our embrace that my naked body was revealed. Rubbing my full belly, my mom looked up and motioned for me to move onto the bed nearby. I had become so engulfed by her presence that I hadn't taken in our surroundings. We were in an unfamiliar room, largely bare and devoid of windows.

"I instinctively walked over and climbed onto the bed. My mother helped me position myself on my hands and knees, leaning my body forward to align my shoulders and hands. Behind me, I sensed my mother shifting, her presence an anchor amid the waves of tightening pressure that traveled through me, urging me to push. The absence of pain felt surreal.

"My concentration remained locked in—making sure to bear down from my chest to my womb and vaginal canal. Three short pushes separated me from holding a baby in my arms as I lay in the bed.

"Beautiful by every definition, my baby had an oval-shaped face, caramel skin, and deep, wavy curls. Keeping with the ritual of scanning my babies that had come before, I examined every inch of its plump body. I traced the tiny toes and fingers, marveling at their perfect form, while those doughy eyes blinked slowly, reflecting my face in their depths as if they were memorizing me.

"I could see my mom busy in the background, clearing the space from the beauty that labor brings with it. She then came over to join us on the bed. With a smile on her face as she looked down at the baby, she uttered, 'Ian.' It was the only word spoken between us before she disappeared.

"Like a movie on the silver screen, the dream cut to a new scene where I jumped out of my car to enter a grocery store. As I navigated the aisles, familiar faces emerged, their eyes widening in surprise at the sight of me, a buoyant energy embracing every smile. 'You look so good,' one said. 'When did you have the baby?' another asked.

"Lost in the tempo of my shopping, I replied with a quick smile, 'Oh, I had him earlier today. It's wonderful to see you!' My words felt like a celebration, a reminder of the joy I carried."

Back in the room with Cliff again, I took a deep breath, pausing my thoughts and words. Pacing the floor now, Cliff jumped in, "And then what happened next?"

"The dream ended. She's well, babe! God healed her; she crossed over safely. I now know that she is all good. She's been here the whole time. That hug was familiar, as if no time had passed us by.

"Babe, can you believe it's been nine whole years? She was my midwife, and she knew what to do. This was the easiest labor I've experienced. His name is Ian." My voice grew in elevation, while energy pulsated down to the soles of my feet and back up my spine.

"So, let me get this straight—you had a baby by a white man? His name was Ian?" asked a puzzled Cliff, who had been doing his best to contend with my raging excitement while trying to track all the moving parts of the dream.

I chuckled in response, "Yes, his name was Ian, babe."

Sensing my eagerness to get on with my day, Cliff shared, "Babe, I'm so happy for you. This is what you needed and had been asking for. This is amazing. I don't even know what else to say." We shared a cozy embrace—my second for the day.

I was determined to spend as much time as needed to dissect this dream piece by piece. While I had received many answers to my questions, the dream also brought with it new questions—particularly this piece about the baby.

I reached out to an aunt who had been a spiritual advisor to me. In my mind, she had to be the woman that Kasey spoke of during my reiki session—the one with maternal energy who was here to mother me in this chapter of my life.

During our call, I told her all about the dream, including the birth sequence. She shared that the baby held a figurative meaning of sorts. As she explained it, I was pregnant with ideas. She did a quick Google search, revealing that Ian means "God's grace."

Was my mother telling me that God's grace was inside of me? And that she was still with me, helping to bring what was inside of me into the world? She had come to deliver the baby and give him a name before disappearing.

The dream had filled my heart with so much light; it was as if the darkness was clearing. The clouds were moving away to give the sun time to provide the heat I'd been seeking for so long. I spent the subsequent weeks replaying the dream, rewinding the tape to see my mom again and the work we did together that day.

While away on a girls' trip to celebrate Chantel's birthday, I had a tear-filled talk with my friend Simone on a sunny wooden deck by Lake Michigan. Given all the time we spent out there together, we named our sacred place "The Library"—a space for spoken and unspoken truths; a space expansive enough to also hold the fuckery that came when the others joined us.

Simone was a friend I'd met a couple of years prior through the many gatherings held by Chantel. A fellow Black woman whose energy was full of whatever she carried in her purse that day, she could bring joy and laughter into a dark space. And also, she could pack enough venom to take out a village of enemies in the blink of an eye.

She was my type. I call her my "popsicles and pistols" friend. We'd bonded through her yoga classes, text messages, and shared downloads about our respective healing journeys.

We cried fountains as I talked through all the details from the dream, enough to fill the lake surrounding us. Before we wrapped up, she did what she always does in a loving way–she gave me a gentle nudge to take another step into the unknown.

"So, did you call Diane back? And what did she say?" she asked. Making that phone call hadn't crossed my mind at all before Simone's questions.

"Sis, I never thought to close the loop with her, but I will now. I appreciate you."

A month passed before I gathered the nerve to call Diane. I was still reeling from the dream and feeling unsure of what it all meant.

"I'm so glad you called; it's so good to hear from you again!" Diane proclaimed after answering my call.

"Diane, she came to visit in my dreams just like you said she would." The scream blaring through the phone caused me to pull it away from my ear.

"I told you she would come. Hallelujah, amen! I can see and feel these things before they happen. Sometimes I feel crazy even sharing what I experience, but I can't help myself. So, tell me about the dream. What happened?"

I narrated the dream's events as Diane rejoiced, divulging the joy in her spirit. "I'm so happy you called me!" she said.

"That wasn't a baby you were carrying. You didn't have a baby. You are pregnant with ideas," she continued.

"That dream was your blessing, baby, and this call was my confirmation to continue sharing what God shares with me. Whatever ideas you have, babe, know that you have everything you need to bring them to life. Your mom is with you every step of the way. In fact, she never left."

Removing the phone from my ear after the call ended allowed the feelings to rain down on me. My skin began to tingle when the resemblance of Diane's message connected with the same words my aunt had used. The synchronicities began to overwhelm me, making it challenging to fully grasp all the wisdom being bestowed upon me.

Instead, I decided to lean into my practice of making promises to myself, deciding that I was ready to make another—a promise to keep going and digging. I had everything I needed within me to do so and began questioning. Maybe I didn't have to relinquish my power to the unsettling choices I had made, which I believed for so long had gotten in the way of my wholeness.

Maybe I could choose again and again.

CHAPTER 22:

Packin' Bags

What felt like pure happenstance at the time—a gravitational pull of sorts—caused my eyes to zero in on an episode about the healing journeys of three individuals one night as I hopelessly scrolled through one of my various TV apps.

They had been selected to participate in a guided psychedelic psychotherapy retreat somewhere outside of the States. I watched in awe as they each shared details about their respective challenges in moving past difficult experiences and how they had grown weary from not being okay.

One of them spoke about the impact of her father's suicide and how their closeness was abruptly interrupted. Another person shared how the absence of his father, whom he never got to know, was impeding his ability to trust people—not just in intimate settings, but even in professional ones. I was struck by their vulnerability and the similarities in the pain I, too, was carrying. I cried as they cried.

By the end of the episode, I went into full investigative mode, googling anything and everything to find out how I could get my hands on these magic mushrooms. In the subsequent weeks, I became well-versed in all the benefits—such as generating new neural pathways in the brain and achieving the state of relaxation needed to access both consciously and unconsciously buried events. There was no ego getting in the way; people could experience an authentic version of themselves and articulate what they were seeing, no matter how bizarre or painful.

Cliff caught wind of my excitement and decided to join in on the fun. I am forever grateful that he counted himself in and shared my intrigue in exploring our "what next" together. Together, we watched countless documentaries about people making breakthroughs. With the help of professionals, these individuals walked away with insights that held the clues to release and enlightenment.

Once the decision was made to embark on my own journey, the universe conspired on my behalf, orchestrating all the pieces. Like magic, I met an experienced guide who would not only help to source the mushrooms, but would also bring together a small group of truth seekers. These were people who had been on their own paths of self-discovery and who also felt ready to take the leap.

Cliff, Simone, and I met this man—Ibrahim—at a party for a mutual friend when a benign conversation about wanting to embark on a journey became a reality. Ibrahim had personally participated in his own journeys and then served as a guide for others. The discussion about his experiences transported us from that party room into another world that held answers to the unknown. Before leaving, we exchanged information and made plans to turn this dream into reality.

Once the date was set for journey day, we had

three weeks to prepare. Ibrahim emphasized the critical importance of readiness before embarking on a journey—also referred to as "taking a trip." He stressed that we should set intentions to clearly outline what each of us wanted to gain from the experience, defining the questions or tensions we wished to address. He also encouraged us to journal and meditate about our intentions as a means to refine and reshape them.

"Being as clear as possible is the aim," he said. "Many things can arise during a journey, so spend time ensuring that you get what it is you are seeking."

I shared with him some stories I'd read and documentaries I'd watched about people experiencing "bad trips," which he attributed to a lack of preparation before going in. "This won't be your experience," he assured me.

Ibrahim went further by making an explicit connection between readiness—the cumulative work we've done to get here—and the intention-setting process. In our case, readiness could be seen in our individual experiences with being in therapeutic settings over time and taking gradual steps toward learning more about ourselves, our pasts, and identifying some level of insight into what we felt was next on the horizon.

Readiness was also evident in the self-care routines that had become the norm for many of us. He stated that this foundation would be beneficial in interpreting whatever might arise during our journey. In short, we had all the tools needed to be successful and could spend the remaining days before the journey being open to any messages that came our way and documenting them.

I spent several days pondering all the questions

that came to mind—most of which were broad and general. What do I need to do next to heal? What is getting in my way?

I didn't yet feel convinced by these basic questions and decided to share my plans with Lucia at our next biweekly session. A few minutes into the session, the words just rolled off my tongue, "I've decided to go on a shroom journey this weekend, and I am having trouble getting down to business with my intentions. What do you think?"

Lucia's eyes widened with surprise. "Oh, you are? Good for you! Shrooms can be a great way to knock down barriers and get much-needed answers," she said. "I've been on a trip before, and it was amazing." She continued, "So, tell me more about what you are doing to prepare."

I could hardly believe the ease of this conversation. Lucia had already done a journey and felt the benefits.

She then asked, "Why do you think a journey can help you right now?"

At that moment, I knew I had been in the right place the whole time. I took a deep breath, basking in this confirmation. With renewed resolve, I recounted the many ways I'd gained insights with her help and how I could clearly see shifts in my thinking and behaviors. Even so, I shared that there was still something untapped that needed to be opened.

Psychotherapy, journaling, resting, and other self-care supports hadn't quite gotten me there. I could sense the anticipation of being close to opening the next door. Maybe this work could help me jumpstart the healing process that Kasey spoke of.

I moved on to state my current intentions and lackluster feelings around them. Lucia leaned in and said, "Yes, you need to look deeper—go backward to see what's over your shoulder. Given our time together, I think it could be helpful to learn what you were seeking in your relationships with men. This includes your dad, men before Cliff, and your relationship with Cliff."

She continued, "Use this wonderful soul-searching opportunity to also learn what you need to do to release yourself from any trauma or pain related to these encounters."

This was the clarity I needed. It prompted me to share some current reflections I'd been experiencing about my evolving relationship with painful moments from the past. I could now visibly see and feel the effects of the release, as if having shackles cut from my bruised ankles, where my legs could move freely when standing still or within a small radius. It was only when I tried to move beyond this boundary that I felt the strain of my fingers gripping that same worn rope from my dream.

This journey would be my portal into discovering what I needed to do to open my hands. I would also learn what I was trying to find in these relationships and reveal clear next steps toward trusting myself and feeling safe in my body.

I could barely sleep the night before. My mind was frantically stringing together what the day could look like.

CHAPTER 23:

Moment of Grace

I sucked down my mushroom-filled mango smoothie with a smile on my face. There would be no turning back after the plant medicine was released into my body. Standing in the kitchen with four other individuals willing to experience the unknown, I made a promise to myself that I would remain open to hearing and seeing whatever arose.

For once, I would just be.

Sometime after ingestion, my body went into full energetic mode—standing or sitting still weren't options. I tried putting on headphones to listen to relaxing music.

The upbeat tunes helped me dance off some energy before I succumbed to bouncing around and making small talk with anyone who would listen.

Anyone except Cliff.

He tried several times to connect by touching my hand and asking for hugs and kisses. I rejected every request. Being near him was far removed from what I wanted.

Something about his pursuit to be near me felt

smothering, resulting in an opposite (and unequal) reaction.

The cruelty I had been harboring toward Cliff came full blast and set the tone for our interactions that day. While sitting on the patio with the group, something compelled me to tell him that I wanted to treat him better one day—but today wasn't that day. Talk about a mic drop.

At some point, Ibrahim asked us to find our own space to let the shrooms settle in. I chose to be alone on a cool couch. With my eyes closed, I saw images of broken clocks, crayons, doll heads, and clown faces flashing across my eyelids. There were also moving images of calming purple, green, and blue colors— something akin to the kaleidoscopes I had played with as a child and consistent with what others had described in the documentaries.

Ibrahim peeked in a few times when my eyes were able to capture his presence. Once, he came to sit next to me to ask how I was feeling and to inquire about the images I was seeing. Before leaving, he encouraged me to stay present and assured me that he would return to check in.

Sometime later, an impulse came over me to leave the dark room and search for the light shining outside. For a late September afternoon, the weather was a mix of sun, a comfortable breeze, and stillness. Walking into the kitchen, I was met with an invitation from Simone to go on a nature walk. Experiencing our first journey together was icing on the cake and a testament to our spoken commitment to support each other in this next season.

Nodding in acceptance, I slipped on a sweatshirt and sandals before heading outdoors. We strolled casually, first admiring the beauty of the key lime tree leaves and the vastness of nature. There was so much of this world that we had yet to experience, and still, we had already encountered a ton of good and bad.

The air around us quieted as Simone shared insights about her relationship with her dad. She realized that space was a remedy, something she needed as she continued to develop the tools to define the relationship she wanted, which no longer entailed waiting for him to be someone he wasn't. Her tears flowed with purpose, reminding her of the power she held. I listened in amazement and gratitude for the gift being presented in my presence.

My heart was numb to the absence of my dad over the years; he had been in and out of my life by his own doing. I, too, played a part in the state of our relationship. Being with him was a reminder of everything I had lost and made me feel like an orphan. His addiction held my dreams hostage. Unfulfilled dreams of having him be the dad I had always wanted — someone capable of filling the hole in my heart that widened with my mom's departure.

As we made our way back to the house, the sun blared, boasting bright hues of orange and yellow. The rays penetrated my skin, prompting me to lie down in the driveway. Simone, shrugging her shoulders, chose to align her body next to mine.

I welcomed the coolness of the concrete resting against my back and the comfort of the sun covering every inch of my face and chest. With my eyes open, I could see the clouds swirling like Pacific Ocean waves. As I closed my eyes, I could hear and feel the breeze and the sound of water crashing against the shoreline rocks.

My heartbeat quickened every time the images of clocks and crayons reappeared. I played with bouncing my eyes open and closed—creating a disappearing act that sent my consciousness back and forth between oblivion and the driveway.

Taking some deep breaths before closing my eyes for an extended period allowed sadness to lay down with Simone and me. Together, sadness and I cried a waterfall of balloon-sized tears as we watched images of broken toys speed across the screen. Faster and faster, the distorted images moved in unison, stringing together a memory from the bottom of that second treasure chest abandoned at the foot of the winding staircase.

My mind floated back to the past—a ten-year-old girl, stranded alone at Six Flags Great America, wearing candy-red baggy shorts and a Bart Simpson T-shirt. It was a steamy June day. I had made the hour-plus trip to the park to attend a church outing with my cousins. On the bus, I shared my plans to ride my favorites, like the Iron Wolf and the Eagle.

Shortly after our arrival, we were split into small groups and advised on the importance of meeting at the front of the park by eight p.m. This timeframe would allow for nearly ten hours of fun.

We were heading to our first amusement ride, the Shockwave—a ride full of loops and steep dips—when I asked the group to wait for me while I grabbed a drink.

They agreed and showed me the area where they would be, about ten to fifteen feet from the concession stand.

Standing in line waiting for my turn provided just enough distraction for me not to notice that the group had left. Drink in hand, I walked over to the agreed-upon meeting spot. Several steps into my stride, it dawned on me that I was alone in a park filled with thousands of people. I spun around several times, calling out my cousin's names, hoping someone from the group would respond.

Disbelief and panic washed over me as I scanned the grounds, looking for anyone who might help. Spotting a uniformed lady, I mustered as much calm as I could manage. "I went to grab a drink from over there," I said, pointing to the drink stand and where my cousins had once waited. "My cousins must have walked away by accident. Can you page them over the speaker so they can come and get me?" I asked.

With a blank stare on her face, she replied, "Honey, if we paged families every time kids got lost, we'd be doing this all day." The confusion on my face prompted her to offer an alternative—to take me to a lost and found center.

"This is a place where people come when looking for their lost kids," she explained.

"The only thing is, once you go in, you can't leave until an adult comes to get you."

For a split second, I considered running away and fending for myself. Instead, I decided to follow the strange lady to a building several minutes from where we met. For it to be so early in the day, the center was already packed with other kids, many of them younger than me, and all of them wearing bloodshot eyes and tear-stained cheeks. The lady signed some papers and wished me luck before walking out the door.

I immediately went into survival mode, asking another staff member if I could use the phone to call home. This was the late eighties, before cell phones were in the hands of millions, and my mom didn't even own the next best alternative—a pager. I knew some phone numbers by heart—my home and my Auntie's number.

Throughout the day, I called both numbers back-to-back without an answer. I watched the clock's hand spin around in this hellhole filled with broken dolls, crayons, and other remnants of toys that had been abused as little ones waited to be rescued. Much of my time was spent staring out one of the two windows and pressing my face on the phone, praying for one of my many calls to be answered.

Every time the door opened, my hopes lifted a bit as I witnessed every single kid— even those who had come after me— be reunited with their group. Just like in the movies, every reunion had the same storyline. There was an exhilarating boost of happiness for the kid and their loved ones. The parents, tears in their eyes, hugged their kids with relief, happy to have found them safe and sound. The crowd's job was to watch and relish in the happy ending.

Their relief countered my growing resentment. *Why hadn't anyone come to get me? Did they even know I was missing?* Nine hours into my jail sentence, I had grown tired of pleading with the staff to take me to the front gate. The bus would be leaving in thirty short minutes; at the very least, I needed to be on that bus.

My requests were denied. "We can't sign you out. Only an adult from your party can do that. It's our company policy."

It was nearly eleven p.m., and the park had closed when one of my calls was finally met with a familiar voice on the other end. I could feel Auntie's sigh of relief when she realized it was me. She did her best to soothe my fears and let me know that I would be picked up. "Everything is going to be alright," she said before disconnecting the line.

Her relief transferred to me. She had always been a lifesaver; why would this experience be any different? Now all I had to do was wait for help to arrive before the police took me to the station. The staff members had warned me that if I hadn't been picked up by midnight, that would be my only option.

Sitting on the bench at the park entrance, I smiled as I imagined the scenes from my own reunion. How would my mom greet me? *Oh, I know,* I thought, *She's going to come with tears in her eyes and hug me so tightly that she'll lift me off the ground.* She'd surely win an Oscar for that performance.

The noise of my uncle's tires screeching into the parking lot caused me to lift my head from looking down at the ground. His Buick whizzed into the lot, passing the two cop cars parked ten feet away from me. Before the car came to a full halt, the passenger door swung open.

I stood up from the bench and started making my way to the car, eyes closed, and arms spread wide. My face was met with a slap. My mom proceeded to hit any part of my body that came in contact with her hands. I did what I could to duck and run away from her.

Several cops had to intervene, placing enough space between us to get me into the backseat of my uncle's car. The police officers stood outside hurling questions at me. "Does she hit you often? Are you afraid to go home?"

Still in a daze, I sat slumped in the seat with my head lowered. My questions were far more important.

Why was she so mad at me?' Why wasn't she happy to see me?

My uncle, in a panicked tone from the front seat, turned around and begged me not to have my mom arrested, reminding me how much she loved me. This is when the stop button was pressed on the scene, and I was placed back in the driveway with Simone and sadness where I laid in a now tear-soaked sweatshirt.

In between sobs, I opened my mouth in an attempt to translate the message being conveyed—I had been seeking protection. My mom had once been such a strong source of protection for me. Through her humanity, there were moments when she couldn't protect me and moments when she was the source of harm. I had learned at an early age that people can harm, love, and protect you, even those tasked with your well-being, like our parents.

Over time, I had grown weary of not receiving external protection that aligned with my desires. At some point, I became my own armor and built walls to shut people out, eventually shutting down my own sense of self.

I could hear Simone responding in agreement, as she offered sentiments of "umm hmm" here and there, which helped me to feel understood.

At some point, silence came to take over as the wisdom continued to pour down. I barely noticed when sadness exited, but I felt happiness setting in as the sun warmed my face. Venturing into a dark time helped to reveal an opening filled with light sitting just outside my periphery. Experiencing darkness didn't prevent the light from making its appearance on the other side.

My life had been a mix of both. The work ahead

of me would involve staying open to this duality, continuing to make connections about how I got here, and defining who I wanted to be—with the hope of uncovering my purpose somewhere in between.

CHAPTER 24:

Golden Teachers

The days on the other side of the journey continued to bring new insights. To Ibrahim's credit, he mentioned that this was a possibility and advised me to keep my journal nearby to capture what arose. For me, these messages often came in the wee hours of the morning or while driving. My journal stayed by my bedside, and I used my cell phone to capture voice notes when my hands weren't free. Regardless of the time of day, the words poured out like water from a faucet, proficiently assembled to highlight important associations related to my perpetual longing for external protection.

My individual and collective experiences with my parents helped to shape my understanding of what protection was or wasn't. Protection was a sense of safety afforded to me by others and was perceived as the absence of harmful situations. Not only did I experience these harmful situations, but I encountered them alongside people who also contributed to joyful experiences.

Ultimately, this made my foundational definition of safety a slippery slope, increasing the threshold for confusion.

Unbeknownst to me, I experienced my first death early in life—the death of self—which brought about a palpable, yet undetectable, disconnection between who God designed me to be and how I perceived myself. Death of self resulted in removing myself from the protection algorithm and sent me on an obstacle course of prematurely relinquishing my power to others, making them more active participants in deciding my fate than I was.

This disconnection, coupled with a shaky foundation created by experiences that were both consistent and inconsistent with my understanding of protection, caused parts of my younger self to never fully grow up. The little girl in me was in the driver's seat, and as time passed, she began masquerading in an adult body, relying on an outdated user manual and the eyes of others to see. As a result, she encountered many obstacles.

She was, and is, me.

Whenever safety didn't manifest or seemed to leave, I kept seeking, suppressing what didn't feel safe, and simultaneously building walls to shut others and myself out. The irony is that I truly wanted others to inhabit my world, but I also created booby traps for them when they tried to take up too much space. This made it harder for them to make choices of love toward me and for me to feel anything worth holding onto.

What a powerful concoction for self-destruction. There was ample space and opportunity for mistrust and fear to set up camp and build a fire to keep warm. Thank goodness the campsite became too hot for feelings, so they eventually left.

The hardened version of me was okay with that departure. Their absence made it easier to rationalize missteps and others' actions. There was another benefit—decision-making could occur in rapid time, which perfectly aligned with my preference to keep moving forward without consideration about the destruction caused to myself and others.

I brought busloads of unresolved baggage into my relationship with Cliff. When things didn't fully measure up to the expectations I had set for my future, resentment emerged. The way I treated him on that journey day was an accumulation of our time together, mixed with the unbalanced occurrences in previous relationships—me leading the charge while watching life happen to me but pretending to be in full control.

Already living on quicksand, life took an unexpected turn with my mom's transition. This sent me into several seasons of delusion, where the tools needed to confront grief were nonexistent, and the continuation of existing patterns felt like the only option. I kept my foot on the accelerator until what was left of my sanity met an impenetrable wall that I couldn't move.

I suffered another loss—an ego death. This death made it impossible for me to ignore the mismatch between my old ways of being and me continuously rising to the occasion in spite of the physical and mental pain experienced. Staring at that blank computer screen, believing that my brain had abandoned me, is a feeling that I hope never returns. Hitting my version of rock bottom became the catalyst for exploring and understanding the experiences that shaped my sense of self.

Bringing these insights to Lucia helped me step outside of myself and examine situations in a new light, generating a different perspective. This further helped me detach from hurtful situations and create a relationship that could serve me in the present—slowly helping me to open each hand wide enough to allow the rope to be released.

But that rope would never be fully released until trust in myself was restored.

Exploring this need prompted more questions. Had I ever trusted myself when I was younger? When did this shift occur, and why? How could I ever trust others without this kindred connection to myself?

While my life had provided several glimmers of hope that this obstacle could be tackled, I still lacked the understanding of how to breathe trust back into myself. As a constant student of being a "doer," I had come to learn the limitations of my capabilities.

This was beyond my grasp, and that's where my faith came into play to close the gap. Until I could fully trust myself, I could lean on God's promise for me. I wanted to trust that He held infinite power to support me and provide unwavering protection at a time when I didn't know how to do either for myself.

So, I started talking to God and my mom often, asking for guidance, for I no longer felt that I could use my eyes as guides. And the eyes of others had often led me astray, moving me further and further from my center. What I wanted now was a different outcome, which meant that in order for that to happen, my desire to make different choices needed to change as well. A shift of this magnitude held the potential to align my chosen choices with my new aspirations.

Focusing on gaining clarity about what this looked like was paramount. I was once the girl seeking external protection from others, and now as a woman, I was seeking to no longer be shackled to the foundational experiences that shaped the concept of my former self.

Instead, I wanted to metabolize these experiences as a means to learn and create a renewed, stronger, and more aligned sense of self—a self that was capable of surrendering to a higher calling.

I believed that my mountaintop was on the other side of this surrender—a peak designed just for me and no one else. My new vantage point would provide the insight needed to sift through my experiences, taking the lessons and truly leaving the pain behind. I wanted to find a way to see that the little girl in me did the best she could with what she had, to make peace with her, and to rekindle our kindred relationship. My hope was that she could forgive me after all this time.

Yearning for peace within sparked something in me to make and keep more promises to myself that were solely connected to my well-being. These early promises were small and intentional, like ensuring that I did one kind thing for myself each day. This could be making a call to a friend whose voice makes me smile or eating that donut without thinking twice. I found these incremental changes to be manageable and nice complements to other supports already in place—like my workout routine and keeping my nail and massage appointments.

I also pledged to no longer work myself to the point of feeling overly taxed. Becoming my own boss gave me control over how I wanted to spend my time. I had to learn how to exercise my power so that I could take the time needed. This meant paying attention to what a "taxing state" looked and felt like for me.

I wish I could say that I was able to take off running with what sounded like freedom. Instead, I immediately felt the guilt gnawing at me when I communicated my reduced availability to clients in the beginning.

Funny enough, they seemed to appreciate these clearly communicated boundaries. The apprehension was all mine to own—and then disown—after trusting my process and listening to my body. I'd been living in a state of chronic stress for extended periods, and I had to become an observer of my own physical cues. Slowing down to listen also meant that I needed to test my boundaries to understand my limits through experience.

Lucia kept encouraging me to be open and to take in what I was learning as evidence to identify next steps.

"When we live on the extremes of any spectrum, the easiest thing to do without trying is to first swing completely to the other side. For some of us, we need to experience both ends in order to find our middle."

Leaning into her advice, I began to notice the signs of overextension, like the twinges in my lower back or the need to squint when my eyes felt weary. Slowly, I became a vigilant steward of my body through obedient acts of kindness toward myself. This entailed taking more breaks, no longer working on Fridays, and sleeping in most Saturday and Sunday mornings.

Interestingly enough, I've been able to provide others with this same level of care that I hadn't until now been able to grant to myself. The effects of this continuous practice cracked open the shell of softness covering my heart, helping to first ease into my connection to myself and strengthen the foundations held with others—a win-win.

The reflective practice of introspection served as a starting point that allowed me to zoom out and recognize several ways in which Cliff and I, both individually and collectively, contributed to the state of our relationship. Whether he recognized it or not, this did not discredit the possibility that he also brought his fair share of challenges into what we built, including the role he played in creating situations where I felt unsafe in the relationship.

Over the next year, Cliff and I had several crucial conversations where we took turns sharing our insights—things we were gleaning from our respective journeys and subsequent therapy sessions. This work was challenging early in our process due to the tendency to reopen wounds that had yet to be acknowledged or healed. These tripwires were everywhere!

There were times when we resorted to our old tools of retreating, playing the blame game, and not listening to each other with empathetic ears. These moments often resulted in shouting matches that chased away any sunshine capable of brightening the room, erasing any progress we had made in trying to move toward one another.

Our individual therapists were influential in helping each of us create and communicate boundaries for how we wanted these discussions to proceed in the future. We made a pact to stay committed to listening to one another, trying not to interrupt, and honoring any newly established rules that helped to reduce tension.

Some weeks, we were consistent in our promises to talk, and others, we remained in our corners, pretending not to see each other until one of us took the bold step of pulling the other back into the ring for another round. We continued this dance until we made another commitment of being on the same team—no more "you" and "me." We would replace that versus language with a collective wish to come together.

Our definition of "together" meant doing our best to honor each other's communicated needs and staying open to the possibility of that list growing or changing. There would be no more matches where we left each other for dead. Instead, the aim of our discussions was to understand and to strengthen whatever level of connection we held at any given moment.

As time continued to pass, we began to unearth another important lesson—our connection with each other was dependent on the critical connection that we held intimately with ourselves. This aha prompted us to each take some time to individually reflect on who we were before others told us. From there, we made space to share our discoveries.

This process helped me recognize that, deep down, I am an ambivert who can brighten a room, hold conversations with strangers, and then feel completely drained for hours, and sometimes days, afterward.

Empathy is my superpower; I care about most things and people more than I care to admit, and I need to be vigilant in how I use this gift to create the most good in the world. I am witty, curious about how things work, and love using my talents to solve complex life puzzles.

Communicating who I am helped reveal what I wanted in a partnership with Cliff today—a relationship that holds a strong, unwavering foundation based on love, trust, and commitment; a partnership that enables raw, authentic communication with ease, setting the tone for us both to share the good, the bad, and the ugly with love. I want us to have the wisdom needed to clearly see each other in any given season.

I have come to recognize that we are changing beings, growing by the minute. Yet, I want us to build a partnership where we can adapt to these changes and serve as accountability partners, ensuring alignment between our newer versions of self and the communicated essence of who we are.

Through his own introspection, Cliff was able to dig up some painful, traumatic occurrences in his life, prompting a heartfelt series of discussions filled with love and vulnerability. He recognized the pain caused by focusing too narrowly on my challenges while disowning his own. He expressed his wishes for a fulfilling future with me that looked vastly different from our past—one where we could be transparent with each other and openly profess our love daily. It was important to him that we heal and grow together as friends, parents, and partners.

For what felt like the first time, we achieved some level of emotional congruence in our relationship. The sun was beginning to shine again, and planting season was upon us. We held a collective goal to chart a new and brighter future that served us both and made us stronger. And for us, we identified a shared desire to start anew.

There was one hiccup—neither of us had any idea what that process would look like. However, through continued discussions and self-reflection, I was able to establish a starting point—taking off the armor that I had so astutely built over the years. The armor served as a barrier between Cliff and me that I no longer wanted. As long as it remained in place, I would never be able to embrace protection from him, others, or even myself.

In my heart, I could feel elements of safety penetrating my spirit, like a healthy need for time alone and contentment in that space, sometimes just doing nothing and sitting in silence.

I loved it here because being in this space

afforded me the greatest opportunity for both joy and contentment to coexist, without codependency. It was here that I could shed old layers of dead skin and fully embrace the renewed version of myself.

CHAPTER 25:

Rebirth

The car's engine roared in the dark as we traveled through the winding roads toward our destination. The windows were cracked just enough to let the breeze graze my forehead, sending a cool wave down the rest of my body.

Even at three-thirty in the morning, the streets of Ubud teemed with people synchronously preparing for the day, the crowds of shoppers just a few hours away from descending upon their businesses. Generations of families lifted and pulled carts filled with goods, to later be unpacked and neatly organized for public consumption.

My mind raced with anticipation about how the day would unfold. The two-hour trek to Lempuyang Temple (also known as Bali's Gates of Heaven) gave me plenty of time to let the excitement ease before we arrived at what has been revered as one of the holiest places on Bali Island. An island surrounded by the Bali Sea and the Indian Ocean, it was a place I had only dreamt of visiting one day.

I would finally get my chance to marvel at Bali's Gates of Heaven and personally take in the vastness of the views high up in the mountains. Home to seven temples, it features 1,700 stairs and a nearly four-hour trek up the spiritual ladder.

Over the last eight days, my friends and I had explored the island's lush beauty and had taken full advantage of the culture's focus on self and wellness. My body thanked me for many consecutive days filled with massages, reflexology, delicious whole foods, and restful sleep. Every morning, I woke up feeling more refreshed than the one before.

The only exception had been the morning of my mom's ten-year anniversary of becoming an ancestor. That day, I awoke with my heart in my hand, feeling everything that crossed into my energy field.

As I showered on the outdoor patio surrounding my bedroom, I could sense every drop of water sputtering from the showerhead onto my face. The cold water hit my skin like tiny beats of rhythm, gently tapping my forehead before rolling down my neck and onto my steady feet. Gripping the concrete floor, I imagined deep roots connecting me to the Earth's center.

Closing my eyes allowed the feelings of vulnerability to envelop my being, and my senses took over. I could hear the rustling of leaves from the tree branches floating above my head, signaling both the existence of other forms of life nearby and the breeze clearing the space with each pass. The comforting smell of lavender shea butter made me smile as I lathered my cleansed body before getting dressed in traditional Balinese attire purchased days earlier.

Looking up revealed a barely lit sky neatly sprinkled with white speckles of sparkling stars. Even a million miles away, the stars appeared bigger than my existence, reminding me of the intricate interconnectedness of the universe, where we all have an important role to play.

Thoughts about my purpose were overshadowed by the physical ache churning in my belly, an unfulfilled wish to experience Bali with my mom—both of us in the flesh once again. I wanted so badly to feel her familiar embrace, hear her deep belly laugh, see her gapped-tooth smile, and watch her high cheekbones rise to meet her brown eyes. Yes, I had found some comfort in knowing through the dream that she had crossed over safely and been fully restored in God's image, but my heart required much more solace in certain moments. This was one.

The idea of traveling to Bali stemmed from my thirst to participate in more mystical experiences that test and expand my understanding of self and the world around me as a means to continue growing. The dream about my mother and the shroom journey both sparked a curiosity about the many ways I could heal from my past. To continue experiencing this state of getting out of my head and into my body, I wanted to visit new places in the world where there is a strong connection to indigenous people and practices. For me, this was about taking my being to places with higher states of consciousness and evolved energies that could penetrate my soul.

Before booking plane tickets to Bali, I had taken a solo trip to a wellness resort in Arizona to celebrate Mother's Day and my healing journey. There I spent three glorious days taking yoga classes, eating clean foods, journaling, kayaking, and trying new modalities to enhance my connection to self.

This was not only my first solo trip, but also my first venture into the desert. I fell in love with the differences in the ecosystem, with its various shades of brown and green foliage capable of surviving with minimal water sources. The air was dry, and the sky was clear enough to see the stars as I ate dinner on the patio. I left that trip feeling grateful for my missteps and the love in my life that I could feel running through my veins. I wrote in my journal on May 17, 2023:

> *My spirit feels calm; I am breathing more deeply, with and without intention. I needed this time, this environment, and these people to reconnect with myself. Honey, I'm home! I want to return time and time again. It's safe here. Healing has taught me how to create protection and safety for myself in a healthy way. I took off the armor, allowing the thawing period to take place. I can feel again.*

Once back home, a Google search of the most spiritual places in the world revealed Bali among the top five. A night full of laughter on the patio with my homegirls led to booking a villa just two months after returning from Arizona.

Lucia expressed sheer excitement when I shared my plans to visit Bali. Her face lit up with joy. "No one I know goes there and comes back the same, so be ready for the universe to respond." She suggested that I spend some time contemplating my intentions and the questions I wanted answered while away.

Before talking to her, I felt clear about my charge—to celebrate life in all its forms—the transitions and another trip around the sun measured by the number of birthdays we have while in the physical realm. As usual, I left our session with more work to do, which included relaying this important message to my fellow travelers.

I spent time reflecting on what my questions would be, trying to hone in on points of tension in my life that needed attention and clarity. I knew I was seeking a professional shift; I had ideas about moving into a creative space. The dream weighed heavily on my mind. What would be the thing that my mom would help me bring to fruition?

Questions swirled through and around my mind, making it challenging to focus during work meetings. What was this thing inside me that needed to be shared with the world? Even when I figured out what it might be, how would I learn to be brave enough to act on it?

As I kissed Cliff with suitcases in hand at O'Hare, my mind continued to spin with inquiry. I had made little to no progress in solidifying my questions and decided that the twenty-eight hours of travel time from Chicago to Bali would serve as the perfect opportunity to journal.

Instead, I chose to watch four movies, take several naps, and listen to full albums of my favorite artists. For some reason, my mind couldn't settle down enough to tackle the task at hand. Something about the heaviness of it all kept me stuck. I was reverting back to my "old ways" of wanting to get it right.

What if I asked the wrong questions? What if I was still too early in my healing journey to know what to ask?

My mind stayed in the procrastination zone until the hot shower water touched my face during our layover at Doha airport. Steam filled the room, and by the time I opened the pod door, I couldn't wait to get dressed and write down my insights.

Acknowledging my hesitation helped to confront it and reaffirm my goal not to rely on old habits. My hand struggled to keep pace as the words flowed seamlessly from my intuition. I finally had my three questions in hand.

About forty-five minutes into the car ride to Mount Lempuyang, I sank into my seat and let the wind lull me to sleep. The stillness of the parked vehicle prompted my eyes to pop open and take in the many cars and buses filing into the parking lot. Seeing the smiling faces of my friends and people hopping out of their cars filled me with anticipation.

From the parking lot, we took a bus to the next leg in our adventure. The humming of the bus engine as it navigated the tree-lined road brought a sense of soothing calm. We were making our way higher into the mountains, increasing the elevation with each winding turn.

Very few words can describe the awe of seeing a temple built in 11 AD. The clouds hung so low that I tried to grasp them with my bare hands. With each step under my feet, I felt the feedback from the concrete moving through my soles and up through my knees. I felt like a kid again, able to sense every inch of my body as I moved each limb with wonder.

Participating in a ceremony with the aid of a spiritual guide was a soul-cleansing experience, where we moved as a unit, listening to her instructions on what to do next. The world around me faded as silence swaddled the space. I could no longer hear the birds or the chatter from the few hundred spectators who had come to capture their iconic Instagram shot at the Gates of Heaven.

When you go to pray, you ascend another set of

stairs to a higher plane where your consciousness takes over. I wept from the depths of my being, without restraint, until my soul granted permission to cease. Any remnants of weight I carried to the mountain that day were shed and disappeared without leaving a trace.

Once the sound of the wind returned, I could feel it wrapping around my body, giving it a cool squeeze. It was my mother orchestrating from above. She was there again, reminding me that she'd never left and had no plans to do so.

This comfort brought more relaxation and excitement for what else the day had in store. My girls and I had planned to make our last full day on the island one to remember for a lifetime. We were on a mission to receive all the enchantment and wonder our hearts and hands could bear.

After the temple, my body was transported to a well-known yoga center to partake in Balinese chakra healing, an approach that uses energy centers as portals to your intuition for the sake of achieving restoration. I gripped the orange and yellow textured rug with my toes before entering Wayan's sacred space, my big toe mounds connecting with the ground beneath the building's structure. My body desperately craved grounding to counter the boundless, soaring feelings from the temple a few hours ago.

Wayan donned a short, cropped, dark chocolate haircut that complemented his symmetrical face nicely. He sat cross-legged in the lounge chair, directly across from the seat he had motioned for me to occupy. I watched him intently observing me and giving me space to be comfortable. He waited for what felt like an optimal time before speaking. His calmness prompted me to follow suit and tell my insides to "hush."

Even after just a few short moments, I knew in my heart that this space was pure gold, where both secrets and truths were often spoken and kept safe. I took a deep breath while getting settled into the yellow-cushioned, curved-back chair. I was acutely aware of his patience as I settled in. I pictured him in the role of witness—that sturdy presence in a room full of people, scanning the environment with his senses to measure the levels of consciousness and microcosm of energies floating around.

Once I was ready, Wayan spent the first few moments explaining how the session would go. "First, we will take some deep breaths together. Do you meditate?" he asked.

I responded with a smile.

"I will then take some time to assess each of your chakra channels and share insights with you. After that, you will have time to ask any questions of your intuitor that I will help to answer. Sound good?"

The tempo of the melodic tones playing in the background picked up, bouncing vibrations from the walls onto my body. I closed my eyes and heeded Wayan's instructions to breathe in for four counts and out for eight. Even from about five to seven feet away, I could feel his energy sweeping over my body, seeking information.

As moments passed, I focused all my attention on ensuring that my breaths entered through my nose, moved into my belly, and exited my mouth, creating an audible sigh of release with each exhalation. The music began to lower again as Wayan began speaking, a few of his observations standing out to me.

"For your sacral chakra, there is good, positive vibration, lots of creativity, and no blockages."

He continued, "You need to give more attention to your heart chakra in the future. It has green light energy, particularly with love; people feel comfortable around you. Be sure to give yourself more grace when responding to any challenges in life.

"Your third eye and crown chakras have good light energy and connection. You have a fifty/fifty balance of masculinity and femininity. It's equal, and sometimes you need that.

"Your throat chakra has a very feminine communication style that possesses power and influence."

Before I had the opportunity to ask the questions I had brought with me, Wayan shared that my aura needed clearing; without this, my energy channels could become like a wall, counteracting opportunities coming my way. "I'm here to celebrate my mom. Today is the tenth anniversary of her transition. What are some things I can do to connect with her more in the afterlife?" I asked, my voice starting to shatter from the steadiness it held when we first greeted each other.

Softness in my heart began to take over, tears building a puddle to be soaked up by the lush rug hugging my chair. I recounted pieces of the dream about my mom and the confirmation of knowing she had been healed—the light that I now feel and want to experience more of. Wayan and I, without prompting, took a deep breath together before he started to explain what would happen next.

"I want you to lie down and take four deep breaths. After that, you are going to visualize your mom. You can express whatever you feel—good or bad. In the end, send her love and light. Imagine she's surrounded by light and moving into total light. Anything else before we go?"

I laid down on my back on the nearby table, slowly lowering my vertebrae one by one until my head touched the pillow. Wayan placed a crystal into each hand and asked me to hold onto them before instructing me to begin the breathwork. I closed my eyes as the music in the room grew louder. The sounds of chimes and rolling waves hovered over my body. With each breath, I released the tension from my shoulders, moving energy into my lungs and down into my belly, pulling in as much cool air as my nostrils could muster before slowly letting the now-warm air seep out through pursed lips.

I repeated this cycle for a few rounds before my mom's smiling face came into view. She was rocking her short, feathered, Halle Berry haircut from the early nineties, the wind blowing through her dark strands. My eyes were smiling at her face, slowly taking in every detail of its youthfulness. My body began to reminisce about her vibrant nature and the light she brought to me while she was here.

Her image then moved closer into view before slowly fading into the darkness that was creeping in. I mouthed my love to her and wished her well on her journey, smiling back to let her know that I was at peace.

The music was now muffled by the tears pooling in my ears before dripping onto the leather table. Even still, I could feel the audio vibrations creating a pulsating sensation that moved from the top of my head down to each arm. There were tingles traveling into the palms of my hands and into my fingertips.

Cliff 's bearded face then popped into view. He,

too, was smiling at me. His dark brown eyes twinkled as his lips parted to reveal his teeth. I interpreted his demeanor as happiness to see me.

My heart pounded with excitement as the tingling moved into my chest cavity. I whispered, "Thank you. Please continue walking this journey with me. Please keep loving me the way you do. We are in this together," before his image abruptly disappeared.

There was brief darkness as I waited for the next image to appear—a beach with choppy ocean waves moving inland. A hazy blue sky brought a flash of heat under my skin as a small figure came into the frame. It was a little girl in a pink-and-white-striped bathing suit running with her arms extended like airplane wings, cutting through the breeze. Her ponytails bounced as her little feet kicked up sand with each stride. She was picking up speed.

I was intrigued by her existence and captivated by her freedom, all alone on the beach. She seemed to be unconsumed by the past, her eyes fixated on what's to come. Even though her face remained concealed, I could easily sense she was grinning from ear to ear.

Something about her was familiar to me. Was she my daughter?

My spirit quickly responded, "No, maybe she's your granddaughter."

Unable to take my weepy eyes off her, my physical body seemed to lift off the table, cradled by the music's melodic tones. It wasn't until our hearts made contact that I realized who she was.

It was her. She was me.

She was the girl chasing me in my dream. But she was younger, happier. She was little me—no longer hiding. Instead, she was out in the open, fully embracing the kind of freedom and joy that only a life lived in the present can offer.

And in that moment, I knew it would all be okay. I knew I was home inside of me.

Fin

Afterword

My outlook on the winding staircase of healing has evolved. I've stopped asking questions about the destination and have realized that the true measure of progress is a nimble, restored version of myself that is most aligned with the season I'm in. I now know that life will call me to create new versions of myself in perpetuity. For being healed was never the aim—finding my way onto a healing pathway was.

Writing this memoir was a labor of love that caused me to reach down deep several times over, get lost in every emotion, and find refuge in my childhood diary and journals. I had always been curious as to why I held onto these gems, given their content, until my mother came to me in that powerful dream. It truly was the turning point when it all began to make sense to me. I knew the time had come to share my healing journey with the world. It almost broke me in two, but in the end, it helped to evolve my heart from being tough as leather to lotus flower strong.

Please know that I am well today. I am still learning how to embrace challenges while being okay with scraping my knees and also possessing unwavering faith in a higher power. On days when I'm able to tap into my highest self, I do what I can to honor myself from wherever I stand. The good news is that I've seen the mountaintop and now have a blueprint to get back if I ever venture on a side quest.

Since writing the book, my relationship with my dad has remained largely the same. Our love for each other runs deep. However, the palpable space between us gives us what we need to keep our bond intact. My heart remains grateful for his ability to still shake rooms with his jokes, for his calls, and for the relationships that I hold with my siblings (and their families) and my paternal aunts, uncles and cousins. As it turns out, my dad was only one piece of a much larger, loving familial puzzle.

My relationship with Cliff is much stronger today. This experience has given way to discussions that I never could have imagined, and it has allowed us to further unpack both the harm caused and the growth experienced in our relationship. We, too, still have our days when frustration sets in and tries to pull us back into old ways of being. We know this trick well and no longer question whether we will make it to the other side of any conflict. As each other's best friend, we now feel more confident being in a bond that we know can never be broken as long as we honor our shared values—authentic communication, love, and respect.

Our foundation has helped our boys flourish in their own lives. JD is a successful entrepreneur and now lives in Miami with his fiancé, the true love of his life. I am honored to witness the man he has become and see his love showered onto someone that the family also loves dearly.

Emory still uses his lungs daily, but now in refined ways—like reminding us of the injustices happening around the world and those within our very walls. Somehow, he believes his birth order was mixed up, and he should've been born first because he's a complete boss. I remind him daily that the world isn't ready for his magic, but he knows what he's come to do, and they will just have to adjust.

Cinco successfully had heart surgery in 2024. My own heart was in knots as I sobbed the first two full hours of a five-hour surgery. This kid is the champ that God made him. His heart is what makes him so darn special, and now I believe the surgery didn't just fix an abnormality, but helped expand his heart's capacity to hold all the great things that my mother spoke of.

Speaking of my mother, she is both with me and not. She is released into the heavens and also nestled securely in my spirit. I still ache on those important days that remind me of her, and yet it is a welcome ache—the kind that reminds me how fragile and beautiful this life is and how lucky I am to get to live it. I know she's rejoicing in heaven and celebrating this accomplishment with me.

If you get anything from my story, please know that wholeness is your birthright, and your soul is awaiting your consciousness to illuminate this promise. For once that happens, it's up to all parts of you to embrace living inside the promise.

Your journey is made expressly for you.

Let my story serve as a mirror of hope, openness, and courage to keep trying until you catch up to your most divine, free self. Who knows? You just may experience clarity, healing, and more joy than your heart can hold. You may look in the mirror one day and realize that the person staring back at you is the one you were searching for all along. It was her. It was you.

Acknowledgements

I would like to extend a heartfelt thanks to Kellen Brandon and my editor, Kayla Floyd—the dream team that helped to make this book what it is today. I could not have made it here without your unwavering support, nudges of encouragement, and brave ideas.

I owe a heartfelt thank you to Lucia, a true partner throughout my healing journey. We've laughed, cried, and learned together. Thank you for seeing me and also challenging and encouraging the hidden parts of me to come out–because without their reveal, the healing process could never really take hold.

This book is for my ancestors who made sure that I didn't keep this story a secret by placing an unshakable faith in my heart that wouldn't budge until I typed the last word. I am confident that their pushes will continue to guide me as I move to share this creation and many others now brewing inside me.

Thank you to my Gamechangers, the tribe of women that help to make this life journey possible. Without them, life wouldn't be what it is or nearly as fun. I remain forever thankful for your grace.

And to the Soldiers in my life—the men who have shown me what mature masculinity looks and feels like—thank you for being a source of safety.

About the Author

Harper A. Bailey is the pen name for Tiosha Bailey, a proud Chicago native, leader, storyteller, and disruptor who refuses to accept the status quo. She has dedicated her career in public health to breaking barriers and driving meaningful, measurable change. As the first Black woman to serve as Executive Director of a well-known national women's health-care nonprofit, she led with purpose, championing health equity and ensuring that the voices of those most impacted by disparities in care were not just heard but prioritized.

Her commitment to advocacy goes beyond policy and leadership—it's deeply personal. *It Was Her* is her first book and brings readers into her world, sharing a journey shaped by loss, resilience, and self-discovery. Through unfiltered storytelling, she explores identity, transformation, and the power of rewriting one's own narrative, offering a voice to those who've ever questioned their own.

Harper's work is about creating spaces where people, especially women, can embrace their healing, their strength, and their purpose. She uses creativity, raw truth, and humor to illuminate the fullness of the human experience.

You can find her online at harperabailey.com.

www.ingramcontent.com/pod-product-compliance
Lightning Source LLC
Chambersburg PA
CBHW021222130626
46554CB00004B/1330